THE STUDENT
AIR FRYER
COOKBOOK

# THE STUDENT AIR FRYER COOKBOOK

60 QUICK, BUDGET RECIPES

ÉLODIE COLOMBEL

murdoch books
London | Sydney

CONTENTS

Introduction	**6**
What is an air fryer?	**8**
10 reasons to buy an air fryer	**10**
Breakfast	**12**
Finger food	**36**
Lunch & dinner	**60**
Dessert	**112**
Recipe index	**140**

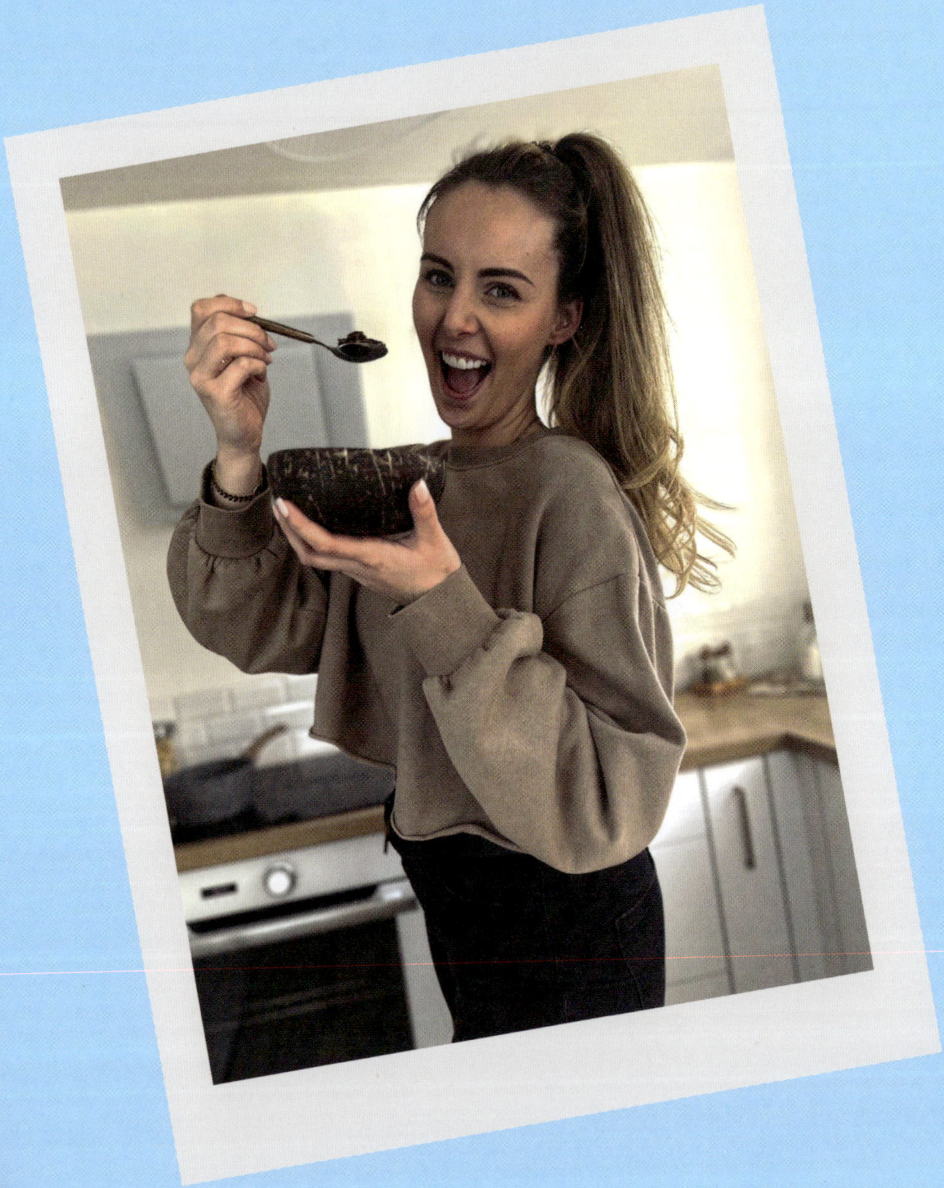

INTRODUCTION

I'm Élodie, a nutritionist passionate about healthy, affordable cooking. My goal is to help you embrace a healthy diet while still savouring the joy of good food, and all without breaking the bank!

Air fryers are innovative alternatives to ovens that circulate hot air to cook quickly and efficiently without using as much fat and oil. Compact and easy to operate, they can be used to make everything from meat, fish and vegetables to eggs and desserts – whether you're cooking for one or many.

In this book, you'll discover a range of quick and delicious recipes specifically designed for your air fryer that are not only simple and healthy, but also easy on your wallet. Whatever your level of cooking experience and situation – whether you're new to cooking, or you just want to cook quickly and frugally – I hope this book becomes your go-to companion in the kitchen. Get ready to treat your taste buds and nourish your body at the same time!

WHAT IS AN AIR FRYER?

Also known as a hot air fryer, an air fryer offers an **innovative alternative to traditional deep fryers and ovens**.

It operates with a fan that circulates hot air, enabling you to **fry and cook food with minimal oil.** This fast and efficient cooking method produces crispy and tasty results, while **significantly reducing the amount of fat used**.

In fact, just 1 teaspoon of oil is enough to create perfectly golden chips, whenever you like!

An air fryer is a **versatile tool**. It can be used to make a range of dishes, including meat, fish and vegetables, as well as desserts such as cakes and biscuits (cookies). It can fry, roast, grill (broil) and even reheat.

Compact and intuitive, this appliance has many practical advantages. It doesn't require preheating, saving you valuable time, and many models offer pre-set programmes that automatically adjust cooking times and temperatures.

AIR FRYER TEMPERATURE AND COOKING TIMES

MEAT:

	Temperature	Time
Bacon	190°C/375°F	5 minutes
Beef meatballs	190°C/375°F	10 minutes
Beef mince	180°C/350°F	16 minutes
Chicken drumsticks	200°C/400°F	20 minutes
Chicken wings	200°C/400°F	20 minutes
Whole chicken	190°C/375°F	75 minutes
Lamb chops	200°C/400°F	11 minutes
Pork chops	200°C/400°F	10 minutes
Pork fillet	180°C/350°F	15 minutes

FISH & SEAFOOD:

	Temperature	Time
Cod	200°C/400°F	11 minutes
Prawns	180°C/350°F	7 minutes
Salmon	180°C/350°F	13 minutes
Whole fish	170°C/350°F	20 minutes

VEGETABLES:

	Temperature	Time
Asparagus	200°C/400°F	6 minutes
Aubergine (eggplant)	200°C/400°F	16 minutes
Beans	200°C/400°F	5 minutes
Broccoli	200°C/400°F	8 minutes
Butternut squash or pumpkin	200°C/400°F	18 minutes
Carrot	200°C/400°F	12 minutes
Cauliflower	200°C/400°F	12 minutes
Corn cob	200°C/400°F	6 minutes
Courgette (zucchini)	170°C/350°F	10 minutes
Pepper (capsicum)	200°C/400°F	15 minutes
Potato chips	200°C/400°F	20 minutes
Sweet potato	200°C/400°F	25 minutes
Tomato	170°C/350°F	6 minutes

It's a **budget-friendly** solution, whether you're cooking for one or feeding friends or family. It's also compact and allows you to cook quickly and effortlessly every day.

An air fryer is a modern cooking solution, and this book features a **variety of healthy, quick and tasty ideas** to delight your taste buds while saving you time, money and reducing the calories on your plate!

10 REASONS TO BUY AN AIR FRYER

1. **More energy efficient** than a conventional oven, saving you energy and money.

2. **Easy to clean,** with just one drawer to wipe and rinse.

3. **Compact**, small models are ideal for small spaces.

4. **Multicooking** is possible for a wide variety of tasty meals.

5. **Affordable price,** with many inexpensive models.

6. **Lower calorie, healthy meals,** as it uses little to no fat.

7. **Flavour enhancing**, as it preserves the flavours of ingredients, unlike the blander taste from boiling or steaming, for example.

8. **Odour-free cooking** guaranteed, even when cooking fish!

9. **Safe to use**, especially for frying, where high-temperature oils in deep fryers or pans can be dangerous.

10. **A versatile daily cooking appliance**, the air fryer allows you to prepare almost anything – from starters to mains and even desserts!

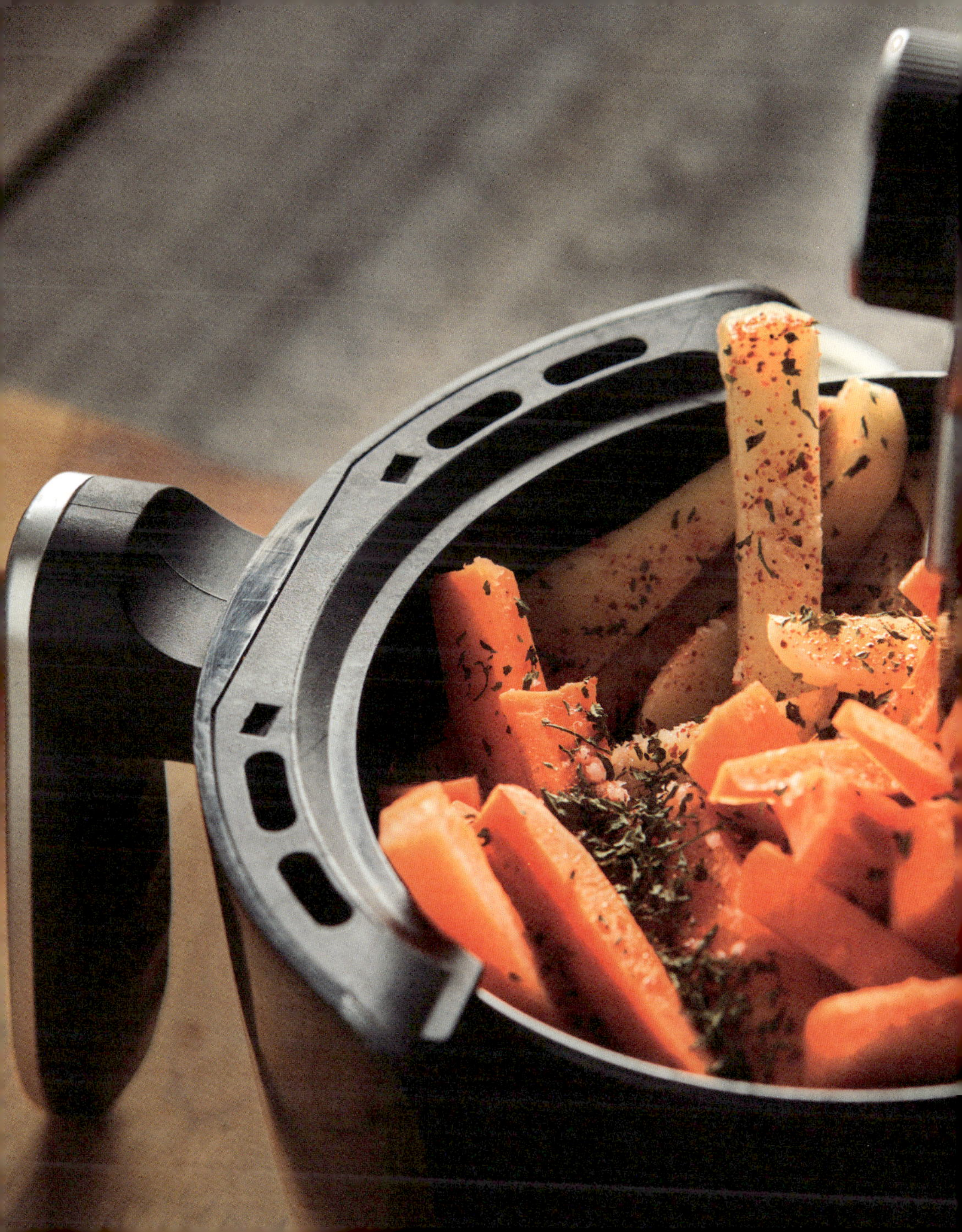

BREAKFAST

Choc-banana porridge	14	Protein granola	26
Breakfast bagel	16	Mini chocolate brioches	28
Chocolate granola	18	French toast	30
Muesli bars	20	Vegan granola	32
Vegan muffins	22	Maple granola	34
Boiled eggs	24		

SERVES 2 - EASY - PREPARATION 10 MINUTES - COOKING 12 MINUTES

CHOC-BANANA PORRIDGE

- 100 g (3½ oz) rolled or porridge oats
- 400 ml (14 fl oz) milk
- 2 squares chocolate
- 2 bananas, peeled
- 2 teaspoons peanut or other nut butter

1 Mix the rolled oats with the milk in a bowl and air fry for 12 minutes at 180°C (350°F).

2 While the oats are cooking, roughly chop the chocolate and slice the bananas into rounds.

3 Once the oats are cooked, divide them into two bowls. Add the chocolate pieces to one side of each bowl and a sliced banana on the other. Spoon in the nut butter.

TIP

For a version higher in protein, add a little protein powder to the mix before or after cooking.

BREAKFAST

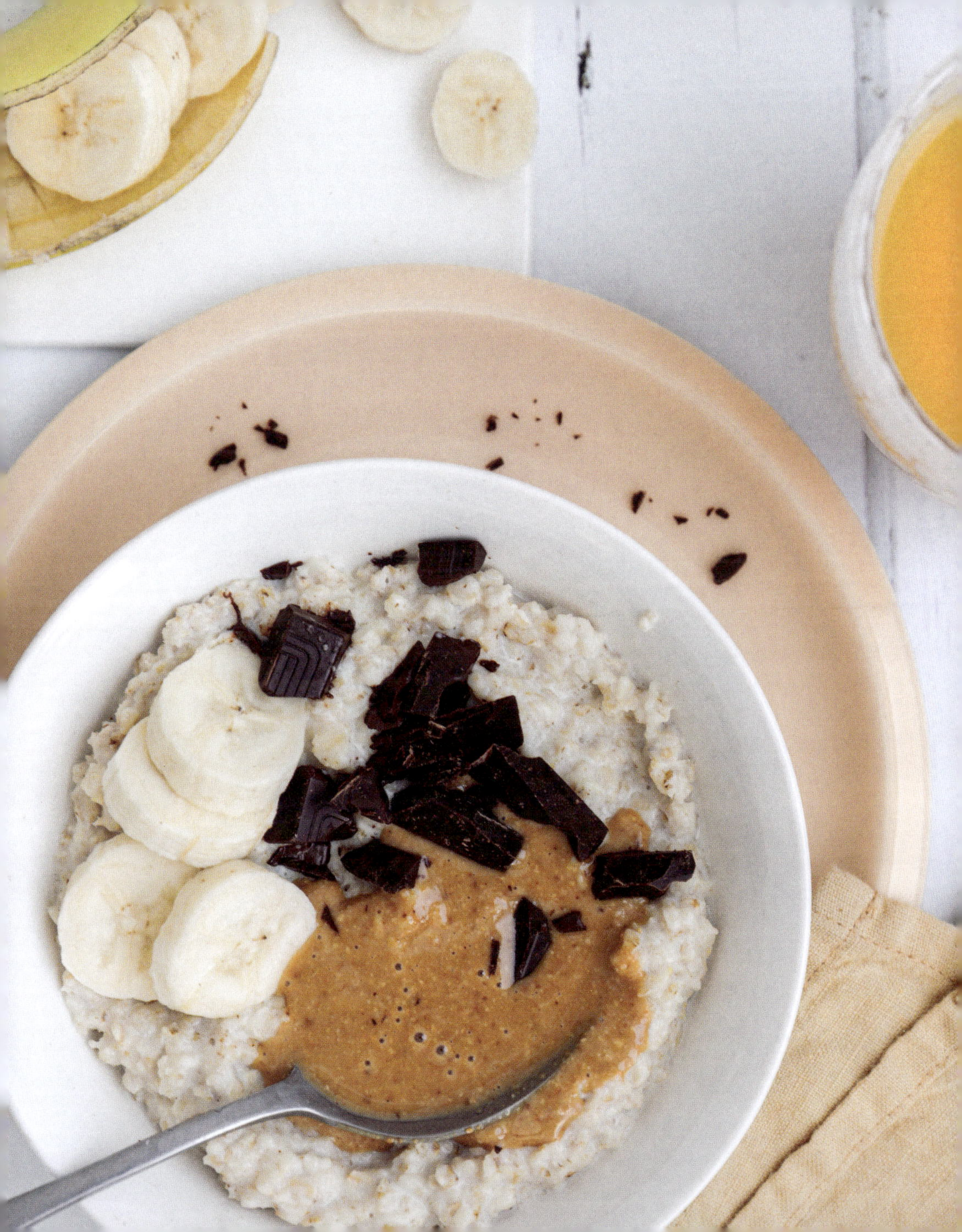

SERVES 2 - EASY - PREPARATION 15 MINUTES - COOKING 12 MINUTES

BREAKFAST BAGEL

- 4 eggs
- 50 ml (1¾ fl oz) milk
- Knob of butter
- 2 bagels
- 1 apple, sliced
- Ground cinnamon, for sprinkling
- 2 teaspoons sugar, for sprinkling

1 Heat the empty air fryer pan for 2 minutes at 190°C (375°F).

2 Meanwhile, break the eggs into a bowl and beat them with the milk. Once the air fryer has heated, add the butter to the pan so it melts instantly, then add the beaten eggs and cook for 8 to 10 minutes. Stir the eggs every 2 minutes, then after 6 minutes, stir every minute to scramble. Remove and set aside, then wipe the pan clean.

3 Cut the bagels in half and heat them for 2 minutes in the air fryer.

4 Add the apple slices, cinnamon and scrambled eggs on top. Sprinkle with sugar.

TIP
Feel free to use any sugar you have on hand, whether coconut sugar, granulated (white) sugar, caster (superfine) sugar or brown sugar. And any thick-cut toast can be used instead of bagels for a budget-friendly alternative.

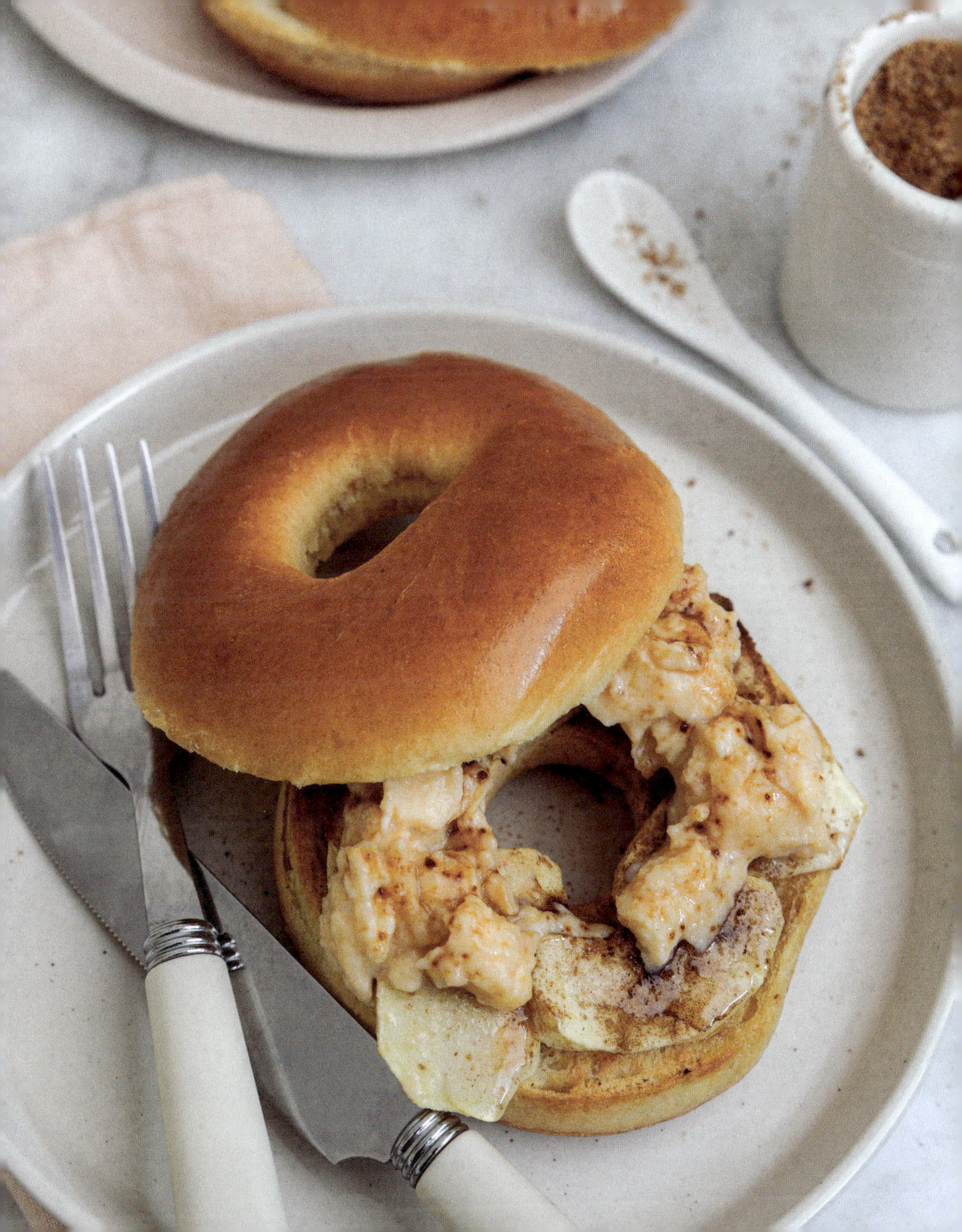

SERVES 2 - EASY - PREPARATION 5 MINUTES - COOKING 10 MINUTES

CHOCOLATE GRANOLA

- 100 g (3½ oz) rolled or porridge oats
- 15 g (½ oz) pumpkin seeds (pepitas) or linseeds
- 15 g (½ oz) almonds or hazelnuts
- 1 teaspoon sultanas or cranberries
- 1 teaspoon ground cinnamon
- 1 teaspoon cocoa powder
- 1 teaspoon melted coconut oil
- 30 g (1 oz) maple syrup or honey
- 50 g (1¾ oz) apple purée
- 20 g (¾ oz) chocolate chips or dark chocolate broken into small chunks

1 Preheat the air fryer to 180°C (350°F).

2 Combine all the ingredients except for the chocolate in a bowl, then spread the mixture out in the air fryer pan.

3 Air fry for 10 minutes, stirring halfway through the cooking time. Allow to cool before removing from the pan.

4 Stir in the chocolate. You can either add the chocolate while the granola is still warm so it melts into the clusters, or let the granola cool completely before adding.

TIP
Add Greek yoghurt or cottage cheese to this breakfast for a high-protein version.

BREAKFAST

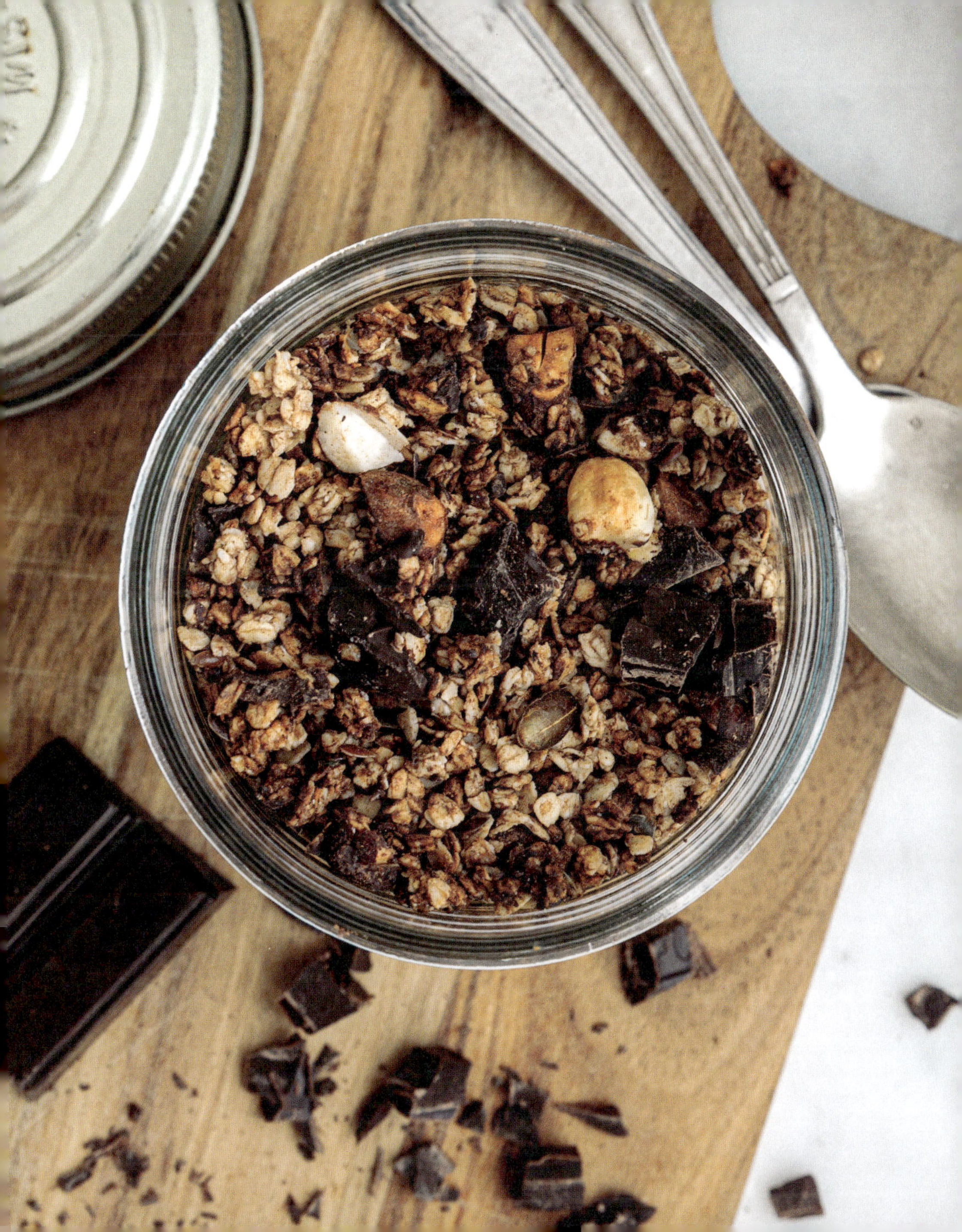

MAKES 4-6 - MEDIUM - PREPARATION 15 MINUTES - COOKING 15 MINUTES

MUESLI BARS

- 2 small bananas, peeled
- 200 g (7 oz) rolled or porridge oats
- 60 g (2¼ oz) hazelnuts, roughly crushed
- 60 g (2¼ oz) almonds, roughly crushed
- 2 tablespoons honey
- 140 g (5 oz) apple purée
- 4 squares dark chocolate

1 In a bowl, mash the bananas with a fork. Add the rolled oats, crushed hazelnuts, crushed almonds, honey and apple purée. Stir to combine.

2 Line the air fryer basket with baking paper, bringing the edges 5 cm (2 inches) up the sides. Spread out the mixture to form a 2–3 cm (¾–1¼ inch) thick rectangle. Air fry for 10 to 15 minutes at 200°C (400°F).

3 Once the mixture is cooked, let cool and then cut into bars.

4 Melt the chocolate in the microwave in 20- to 30-second bursts. Drizzle the melted chocolate over the bars, then let set before eating or storing.

TIP
Almost any nut that is affordable can be used in place of hazelnuts and almonds. Apple purée is available in the canned section of the supermarket, or can be made by cooking down peeled apples until very soft and then puréeing with a stick blender.

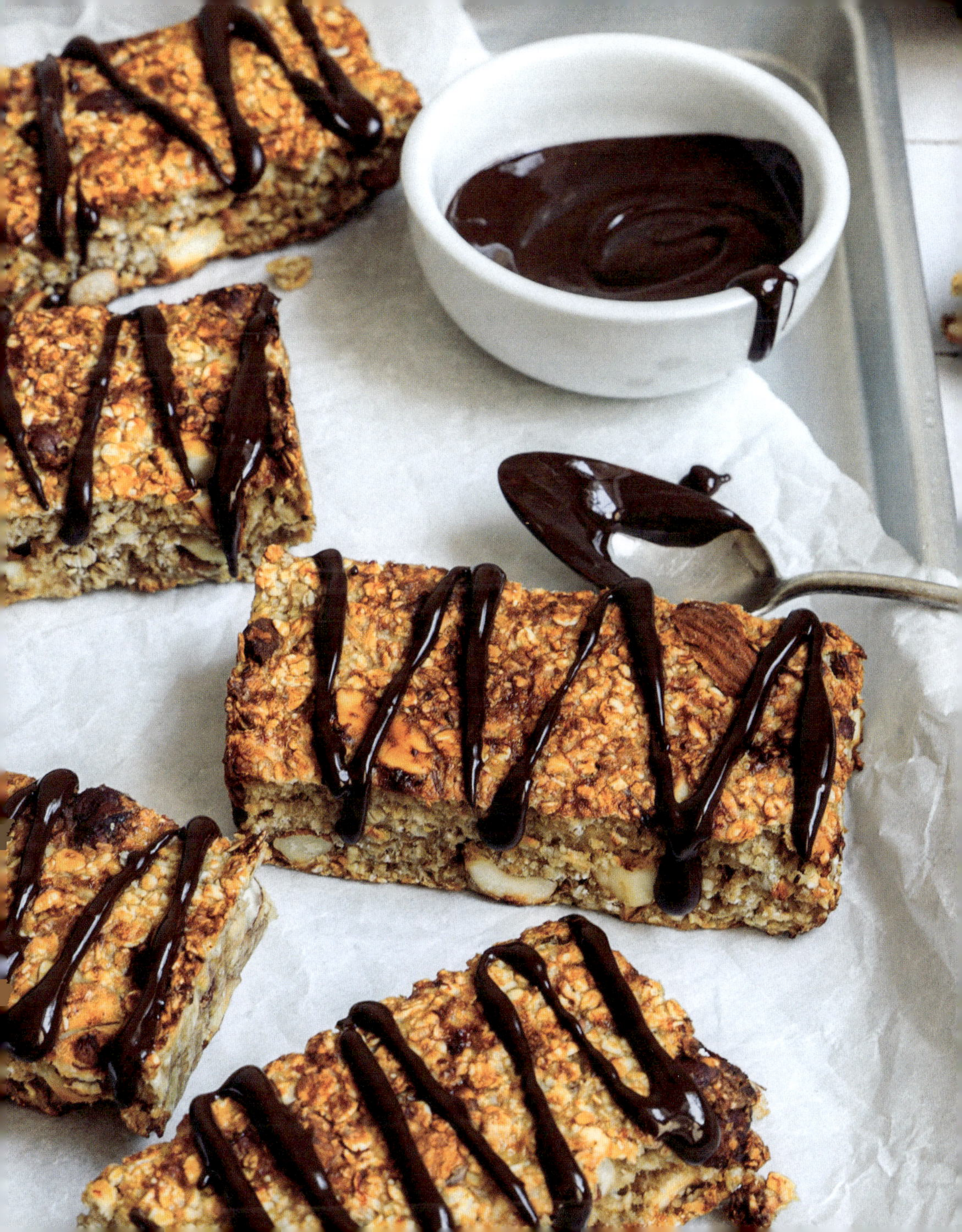

MAKES 4 - EASY - PREPARATION 15 MINUTES - COOKING 20 MINUTES

VEGAN MUFFINS

- 50 g (1¾ oz) plain (all-purpose) flour
- 20 g (¾ oz) granulated (white) sugar
- ¾ teaspoon vanilla sugar, or an extra ¾ teaspoon granulated (white) sugar with ¼ teaspoon vanilla extract
- 1½ tablespoons sunflower or vegetable oil
- 1 heaped teaspoon baking powder
- 50 ml (1¾ fl oz) plant-based milk
- 4-8 teaspoons dark or vegan chocolate chips (depending on how much chocolate you want in your muffins)

1 In a bowl, mix all the ingredients except the chocolate. Once mixed, add the chocolate chips and pour the mixture into four silicone or paper muffin cases or ramekins.

2 Bake in the air fryer for 20 minutes at 170°C (350°F).

TIP

Often replacing the eggs is all it takes to make a recipe vegan. Here are some ingredients that can replace 1 egg:

- 100 g (3½ oz) apple purée
- 100 g (3½ oz) plant-based yoghurt
- 60 g (2¼ oz) aquafaba (liquid from canned chickpeas)
- 50 g (1¾ oz) silken tofu
- 60 g (2¼ oz) nut butter

BREAKFAST

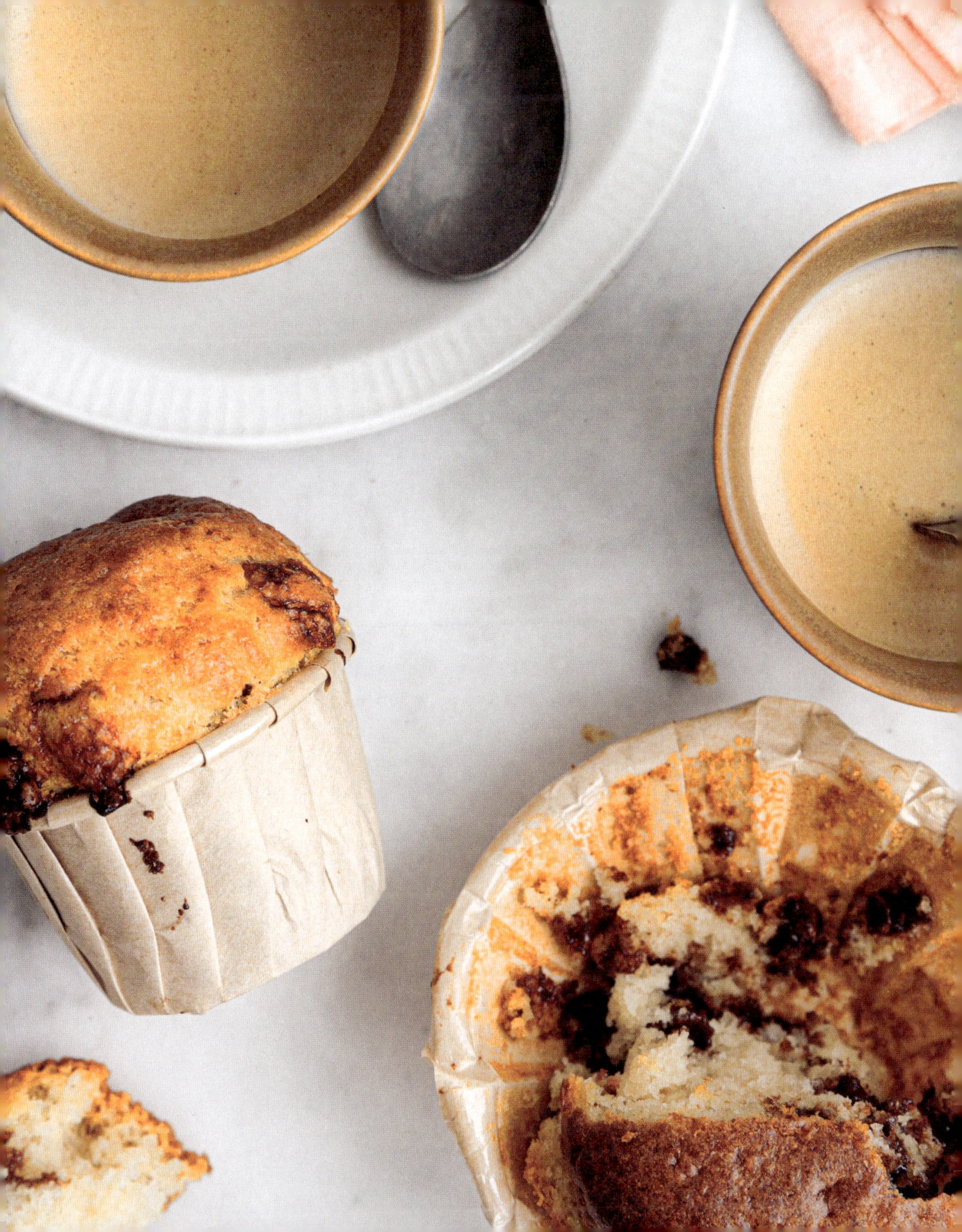

SERVES 2 - EASY - PREPARATION 1 MINUTE - COOKING 6 MINUTES

BOILED EGGS

- 2 whole eggs
- Salt and black pepper

1 Place the whole eggs (still in their shells) in the air fryer basket and cook for 6 minutes at 170°C (350°F).

2 Place the eggs in egg cups and remove the top of the shell just before serving. Season with salt and pepper and enjoy.

TIP

For a balanced breakfast, serve the eggs with wholegrain or multigrain toast spread with nut butter or good quality butter, and some fruit and/or vegetables.

BREAKFAST

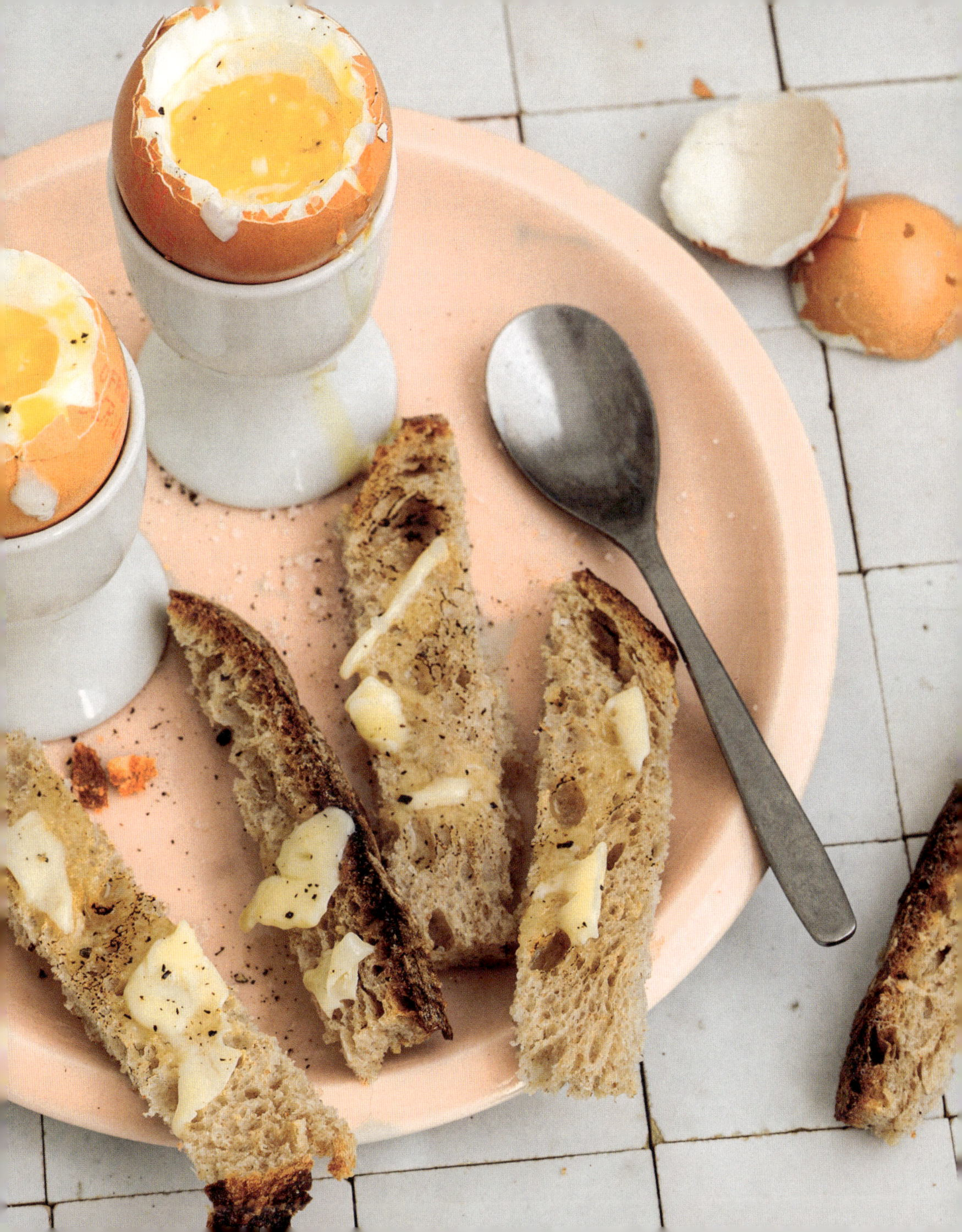

SERVES 2 - EASY - PREPARATION 5 MINUTES - COOKING 10 MINUTES

PROTEIN GRANOLA

- 50 g (1¾ oz) rolled or porridge oats
- 40 g (1½ oz) spelt flakes
- 50 g (1¾ oz) soy protein crispies or puffed quinoa
- 1 tablespoon hazelnuts
- 1 tablespoon almonds
- 20 g (¾ oz) chocolate chips
- 1 tablespoon honey
- 1 teaspoon linseeds
- 1 teaspoon pumpkin seeds (pepitas)

1 Preheat the air fryer to 180°C (350°F).

2 In a bowl, mix all the ingredients together. Spread the mixture out in the air fryer pan or line the air fryer basket with baking paper and then spread the granola on top.

3 Air fry for 10 minutes, stirring halfway through the cooking time. Allow the granola to cool before removing.

TIP

Try buying grains and seeds from a wholefoods shop that lets you pay by weight, so you don't need to buy more than required.

BREAKFAST

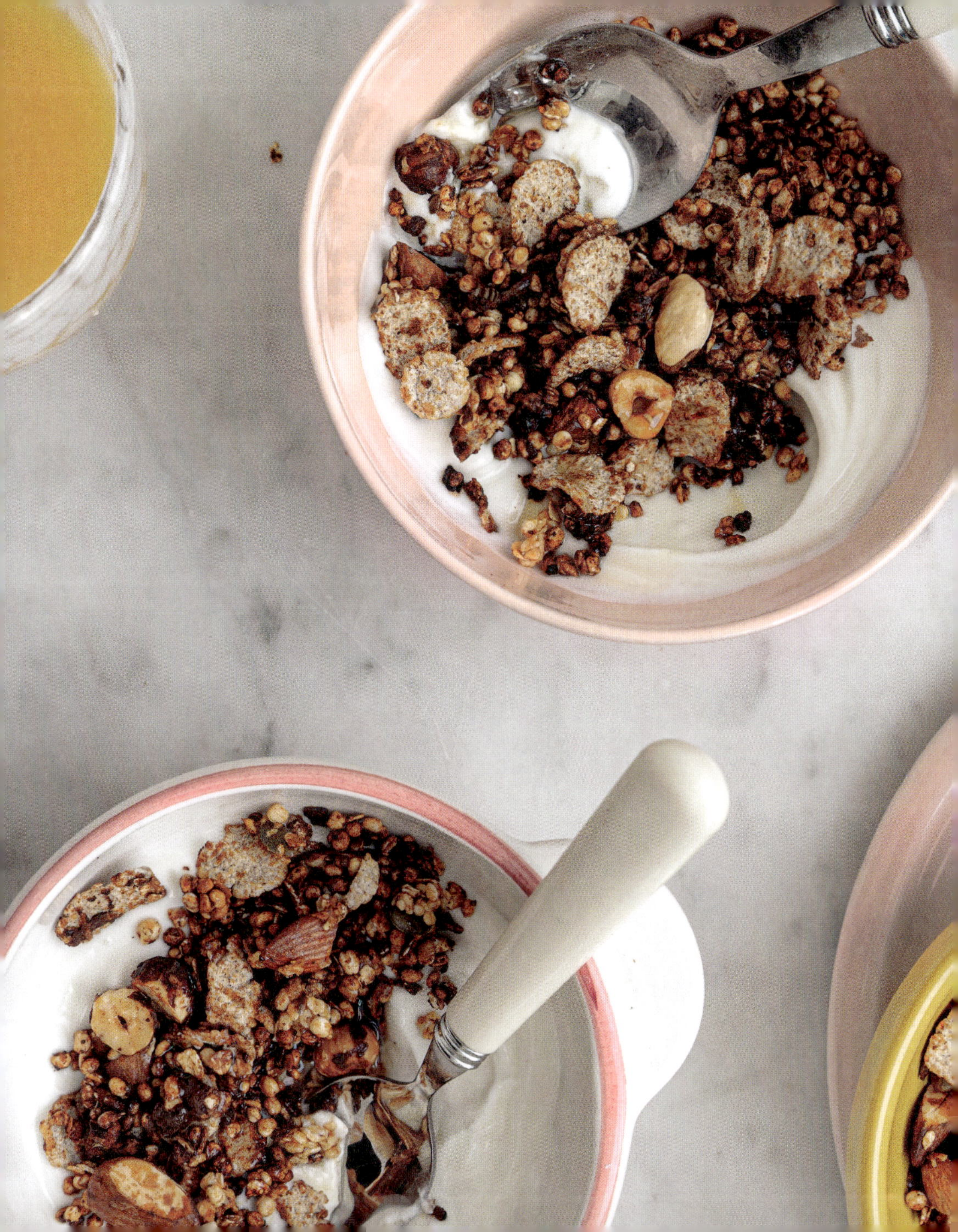

MAKES 2–4 - MEDIUM - PREPARATION 20 MINUTES - COOKING 15 MINUTES

MINI CHOCOLATE BRIOCHES

- 1 egg
- 70 g (2½ oz) Greek yoghurt or a smooth, creamy ricotta
- 100 g (3½ oz) plain (all-purpose) flour, plus 20 g (¾ oz) to shape the brioche
- 20 g (¾ oz) granulated (white) sugar
- 1 teaspoon baking powder
- 20 g (¾ oz) chocolate chips

1 In a bowl, mix the egg with the yoghurt or ricotta, then add the flour, sugar, baking powder and chocolate chips.

2 Shape two round mini brioches or four smaller ones, using a little flour to prevent them from sticking to your fingers.

3 Bake for 15 minutes at 180°C (350°F) in the air fryer pan.

TIP
You could replace the chocolate chips with 20 g (¾ oz) crushed hazelnuts or almonds.

BREAKFAST

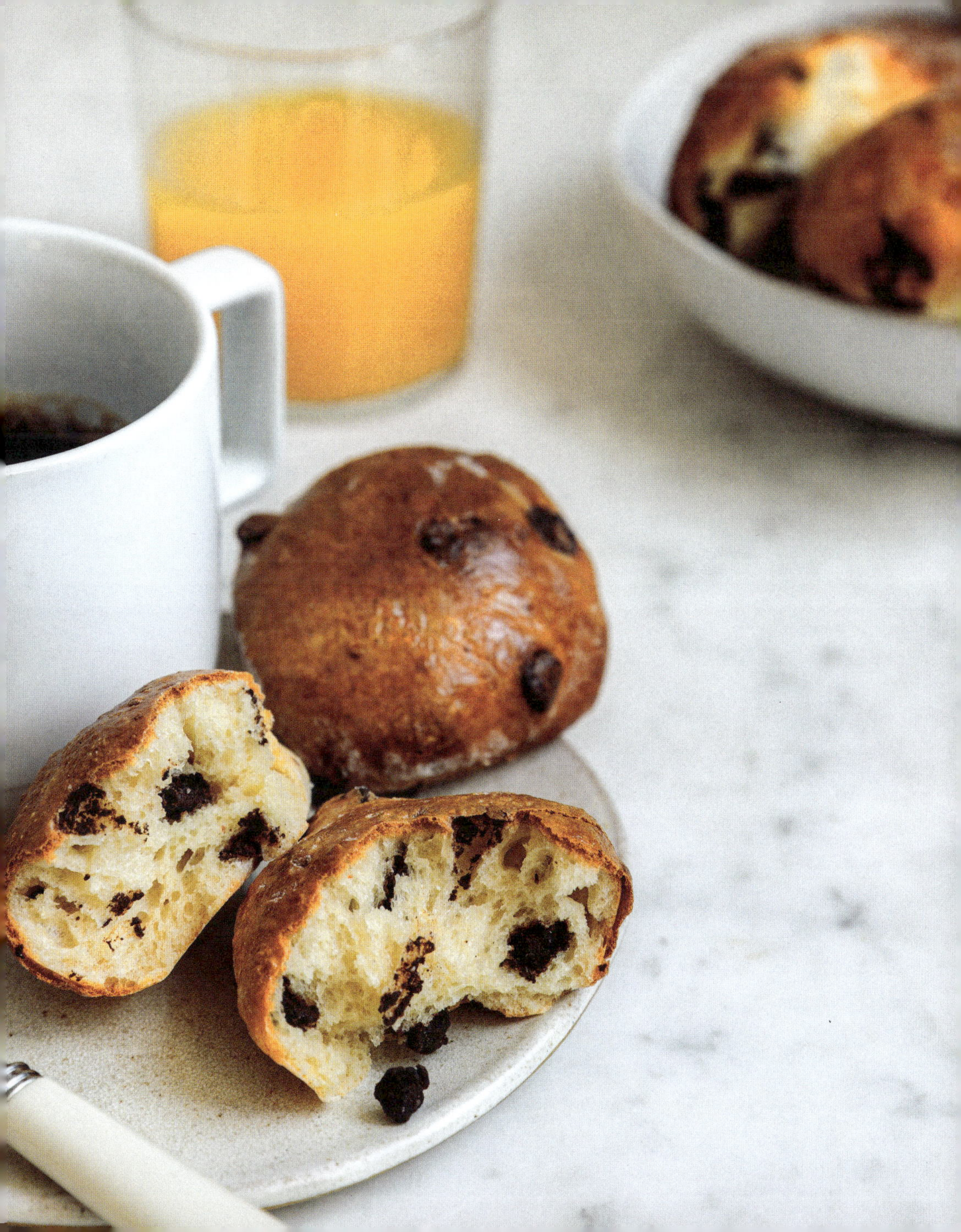

SERVES 2 - EASY - PREPARATION 10 MINUTES - COOKING 7 MINUTES

FRENCH TOAST

- 4 eggs
- 50 ml (1¾ fl oz) milk
- 30 g (1 oz) granulated (white) sugar
- Ground cinnamon or vanilla extract or vanilla sugar, to taste (optional)
- 150 g (5½ oz) stale bread, sliced
- Chopped fruit, to serve

1. In a bowl, beat the eggs with the milk and sugar, as well as the cinnamon or vanilla, if using.

2. Soak the pieces of stale bread in this mixture and place them in the air fryer pan.

3. Bake for 5 minutes at 200°C (400°F), then turn the bread over and cook for another 2 minutes. Add some chopped seasonal fruit to decorate your French toast.

TIP
If you don't have stale bread, toast your bread first so it doesn't go soggy while cooking. Drizzle with maple syrup for a gourmet version.

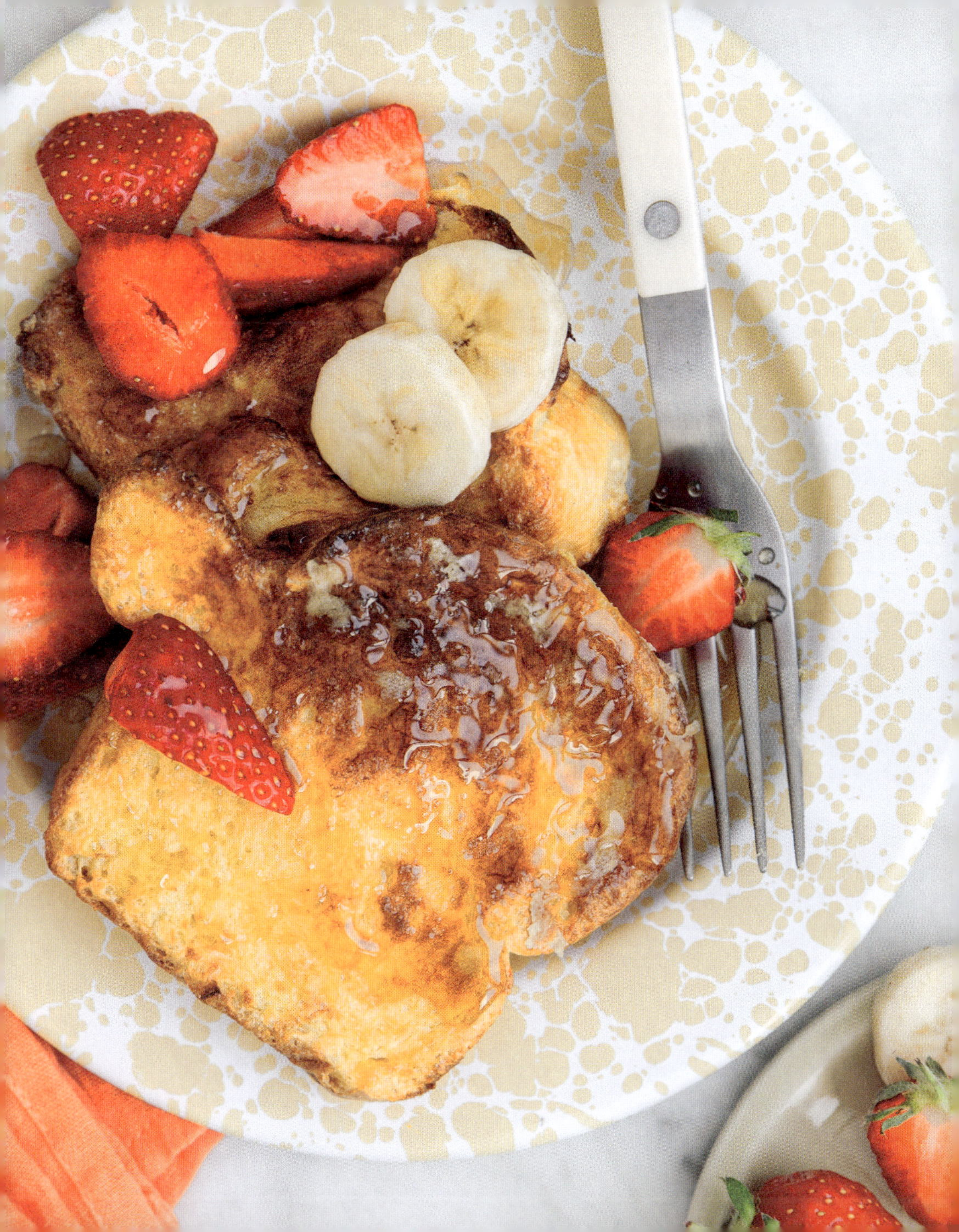

SERVES 2 - EASY - PREPARATION 5 MINUTES - COOKING 10 MINUTES

VEGAN GRANOLA

- 100 g (3½ oz) rolled or porridge oats
- 20 g (¾ oz) nut butter of your choice
- 1 teaspoon maple syrup or golden syrup
- 1 teaspoon vanilla extract
- 70 g (2½ oz) apple purée

1 Preheat the air fryer to 180°C (350°F).

2 Mix all the ingredients together in a bowl. Spread the mixture out in the air fryer pan or line the air fryer basket with baking paper and then spread the granola on top.

3 Air fry for 10 minutes, stirring halfway through the cooking time. Allow the granola to cool before removing.

TIP

Add any of your favourite ingredients, such as dried fruits, cranberries, nuts or seeds. Apple purée is available in the canned section of the supermarket, or can be made by cooking down peeled apples until very soft and then puréeing with a stick blender.

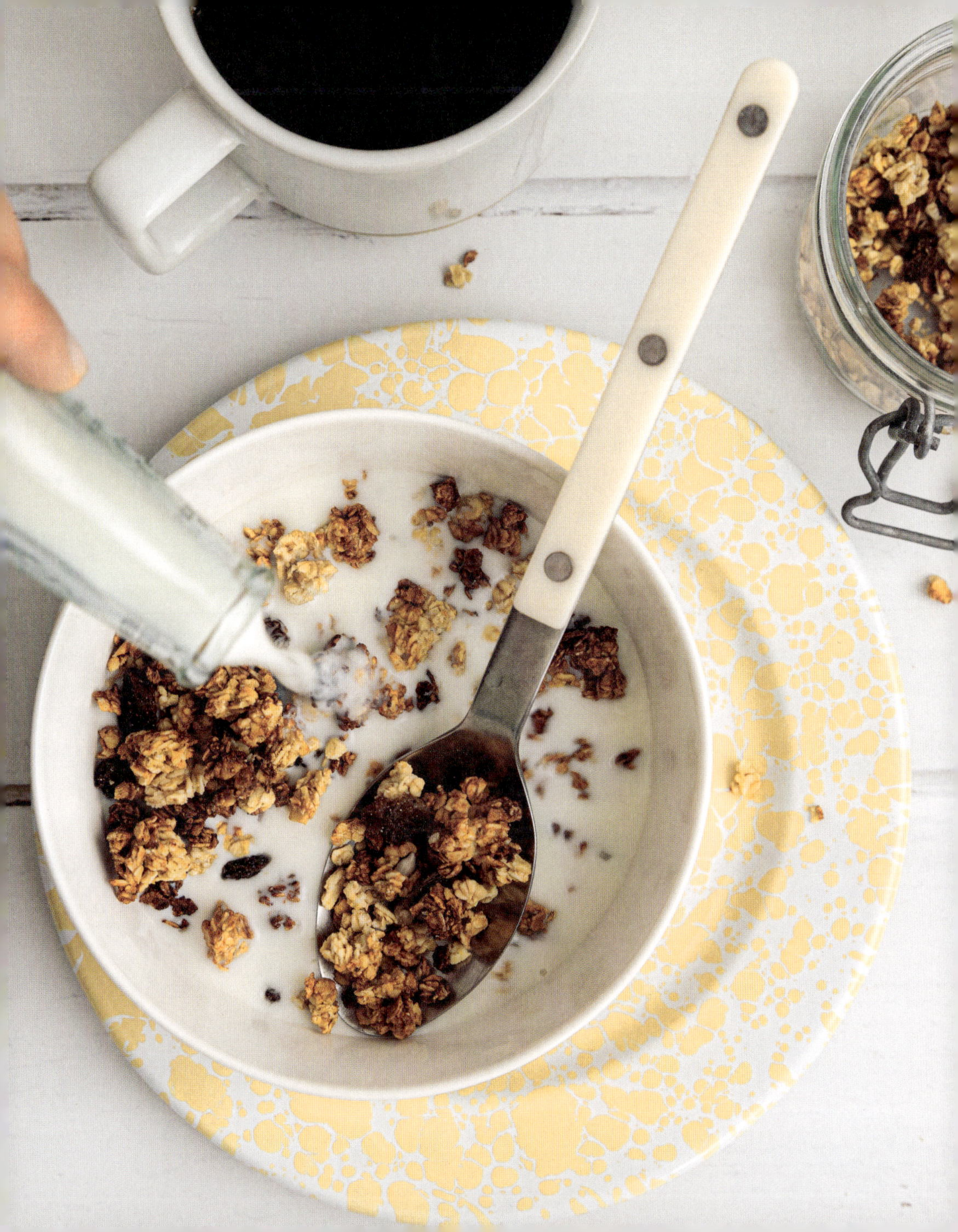

SERVES 2 - EASY - PREPARATION 5 MINUTES - COOKING 10 MINUTES

MAPLE GRANOLA

- 100 g (3½ oz) rolled or porridge oats
- 30 g (1 oz) seeds or nuts of your choice, such as linseeds, pumpkin seeds (pepitas), walnuts, hazelnuts and almonds
- 1 teaspoon coconut oil
- 1 teaspoon maple syrup or honey
- Dried fruit, to taste (optional)

1 Preheat the air fryer to 180°C (350°F).

2 Mix all the ingredients together. Spread the mixture out in the air fryer pan or line the air fryer basket with baking paper and then spread the granola on top.

3 Cook for 10 minutes, stirring halfway through the cooking time. Allow to cool before removing.

TIP
You can add a serve of yoghurt or cottage cheese to this granola to make a quick dessert.

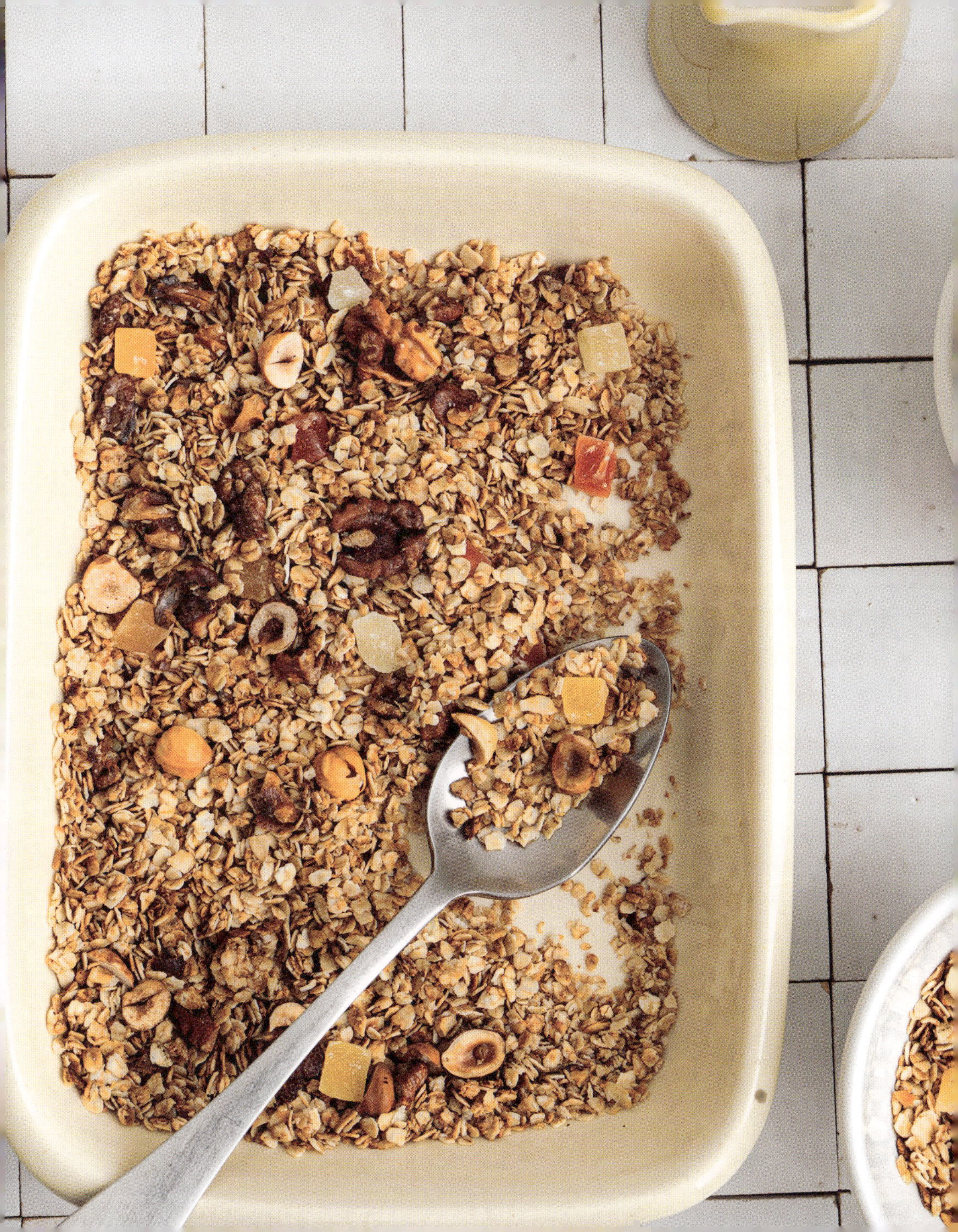

FINGER FOOD

Potato crisps	**38**	Tuna triangles	**50**
Chicken parcels	**40**	Mini pizza baguettes	**52**
Cheesy breadsticks	**42**	Baked Camembert	**54**
Onion rings	**44**	Salted popcorn	**56**
Pumpkin bites	**46**	Vegetable spring rolls	**58**
Mozza sticks	**48**		

SERVES 2 - EASY - PREPARATION 30 MINUTES - COOKING 30 MINUTES

POTATO CRISPS

- 2 large potatoes
- 1 sweet potato
- 1 tablespoon sunflower or vegetable oil
- Salt

1 Carefully cut the potatoes and sweet potato into very thin slices (using a mandolin if you have one, or a sharp knife).

2 Place the slices in a bowl filled with cold water and soak for 20 minutes. Drain and dry the slices thoroughly.

3 Place the potato slices in the air fryer basket (it's fine if they overlap). Toss with the oil and cook for 20 minutes at 180°C (350°F), tossing well every 5 to 10 minutes. After 20 minutes, remove any crisps that are cooked and golden and cook any remaining crisps for 5 to 10 more minutes. Season with salt when they're cooked.

TIP
Serve with a scattering of parsley if you like – it's rich in iron.

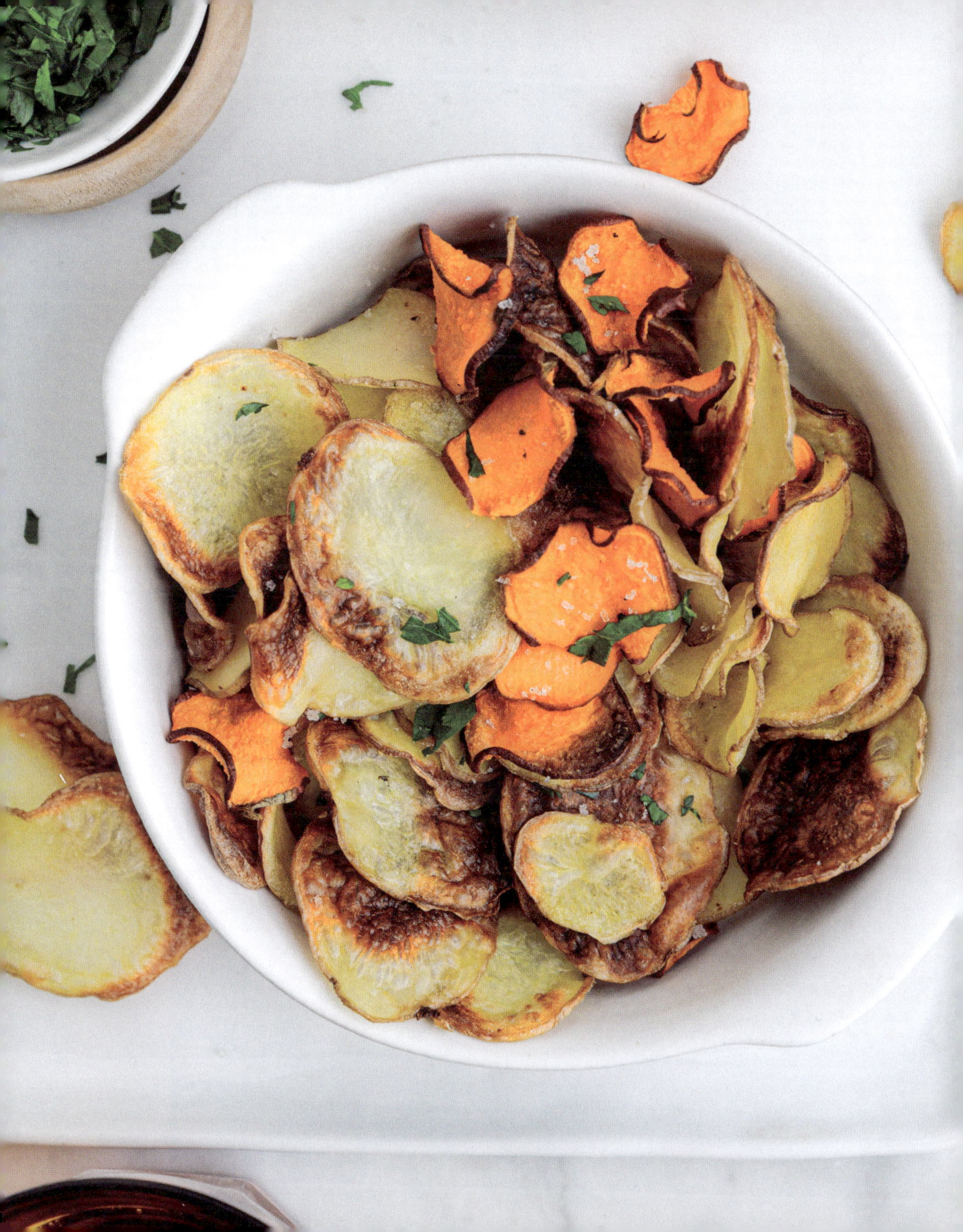

MAKES 8 - MEDIUM - PREPARATION 20 MINUTES - COOKING 10 MINUTES

CHICKEN PARCELS

- 150 g (5½ oz) chicken, finely chopped
- ½ onion, peeled and finely diced
- Spray oil
- 1 tablespoon double (heavy) cream or a smooth, creamy ricotta
- 1 tablespoon curry powder
- Salt and black pepper
- 4 sheets brik or filo (phyllo) pastry
- Melted butter (optional)
- Sunflower or vegetable oil or 1 egg, for brushing
- Lime wedges, to serve

1 Brown the chicken and onion in a lightly oiled frying pan over a low heat. Once cooked, add the cream and curry powder. Stir, season with salt and pepper and turn off the heat.

2 Cut the pastry sheets in half. If using brik pastry, fold the rounded edge over to the other edge to make a rectangle. If using filo pastry, brush with melted butter. Place a dollop of the filling mixture at the bottom of each piece of pastry and fold over diagonally to form a triangle. Continue folding the parcel in a triangle shape to the end.

3 Brush each parcel with a little melted butter, oil or beaten egg using a pastry brush. Cook in the air fryer for 10 minutes at 180°C (350°F). Serve with lime wedges.

TIP
For more tender and tastier chicken, you can marinate it in a little oil with the curry powder and cream before cooking.

FINGER FOOD

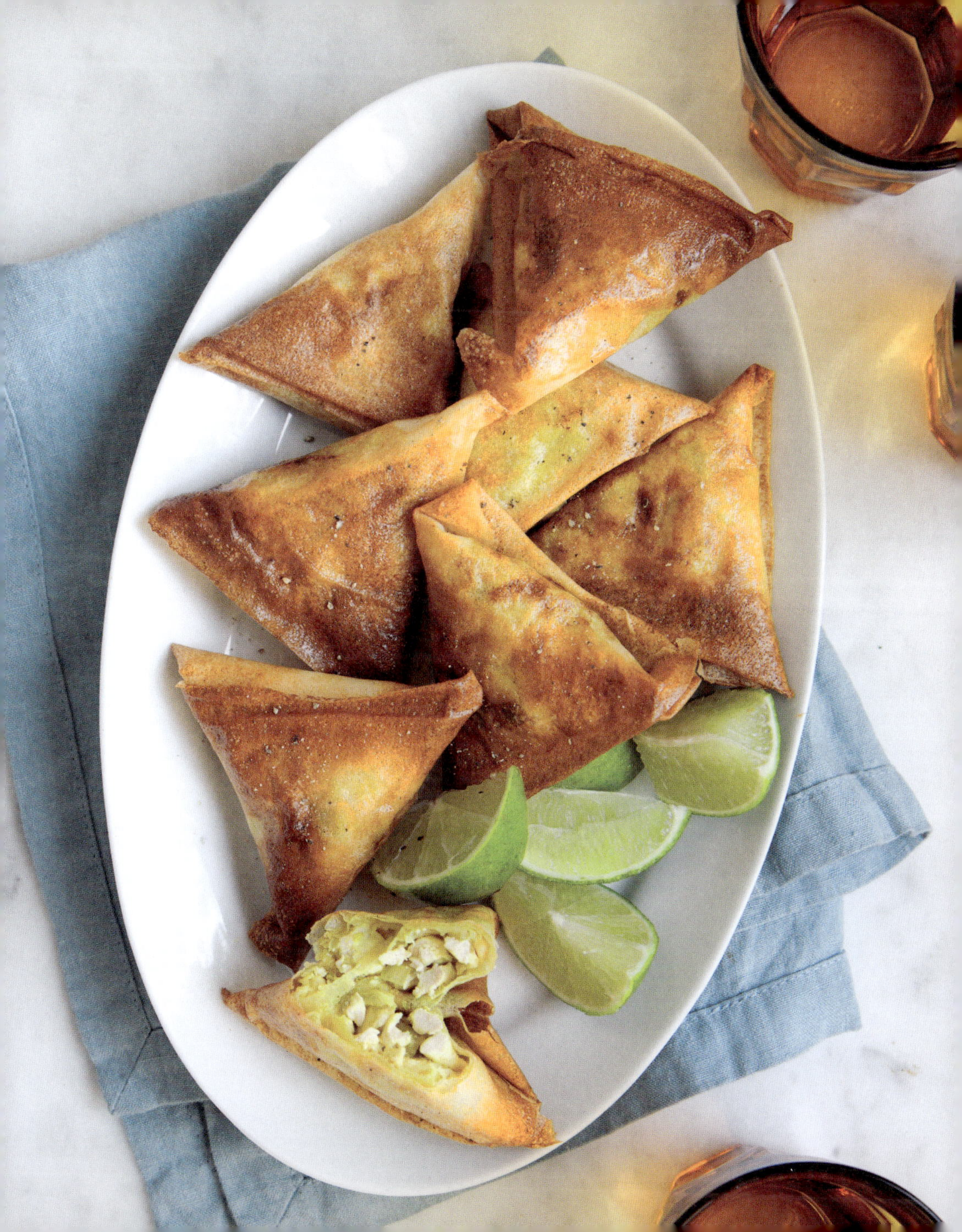

MAKES ABOUT 15 - EASY - PREPARATION 10 MINUTES - COOKING 10 MINUTES

CHEESY BREADSTICKS

- ½ sheet puff pastry
- 1 egg, beaten
- 50 g (1¾ oz) Cheddar cheese, grated
- Sesame seeds, for decorating

1 Cut the puff pastry sheet into 1 cm (½ inch) wide strips (about 15 strips, depending on the size of your pastry sheet).

2 Twist the strips. Brush the strips with beaten egg and sprinkle with the grated Cheddar and sesame seeds.

3 Cook in the air fryer for 10 minutes at 180°C (350°F).

TIP
There are endless variations on this recipe. You can sprinkle the pastry with mixed herbs, rosemary, tomato passata (puréed tomatoes), mozzarella cheese or any topping you like.

FINGER FOOD

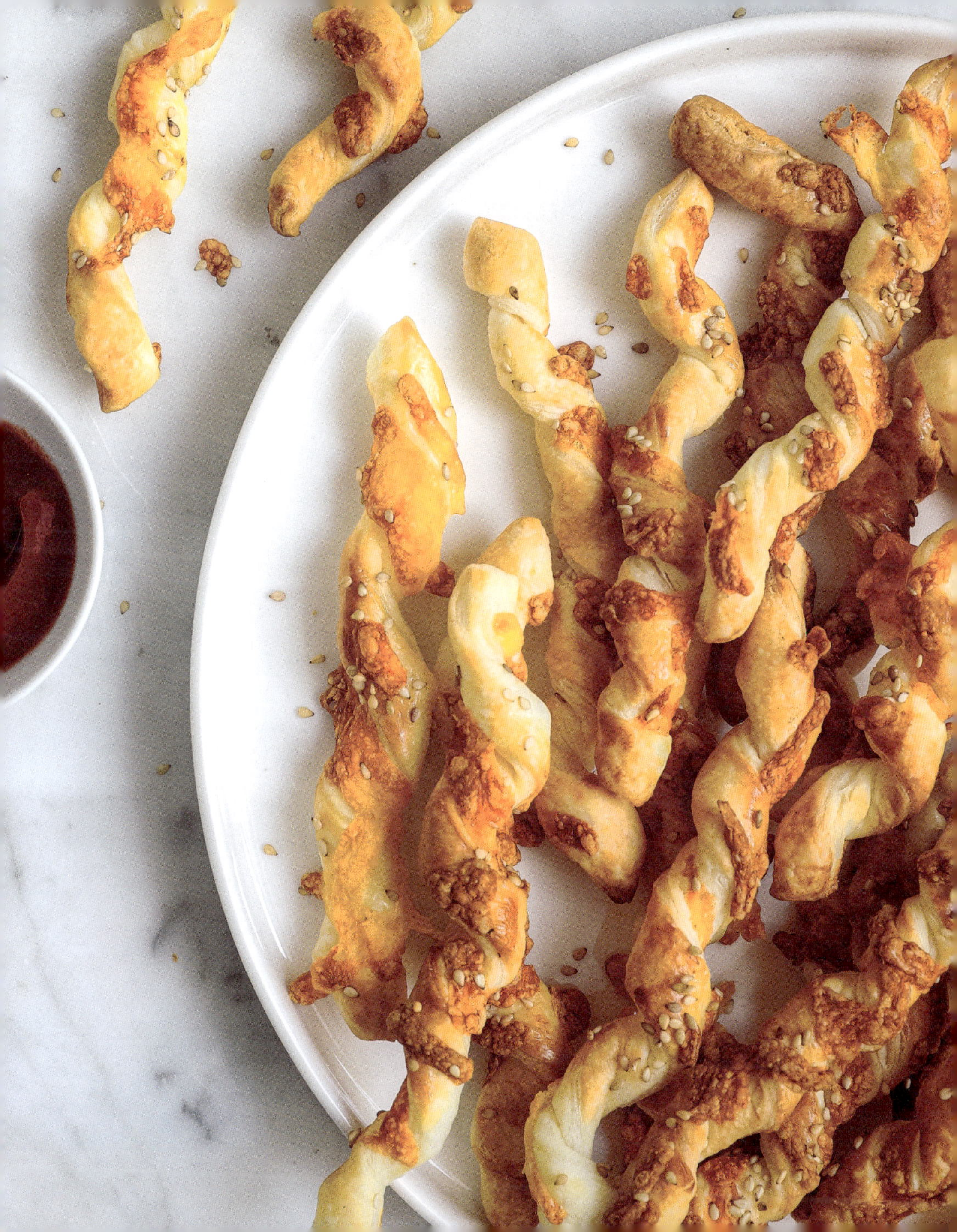

SERVES 2 - MEDIUM - PREPARATION 15 MINUTES - COOKING 15 MINUTES

ONION RINGS

- 70 g (2½ oz) plain (all-purpose) flour
- 1 teaspoon paprika
- 1 teaspoon salt
- 1 teaspoon black pepper
- 70 ml (2¼ fl oz) water
- 50 g (1¾ oz) breadcrumbs
- 1 onion, peeled
- 1 teaspoon sunflower or vegetable oil

1 In a bowl, combine the flour with the paprika, salt and pepper. Gradually add the water, mixing until a slightly runny batter forms. Pour the breadcrumbs into a separate bowl and set aside.

2 Peel the onion, cut it into thick slices and separate the rings. Dip the slices one at a time in the batter, then the breadcrumbs.

3 Place the slices in the air fryer basket, toss in the oil and cook for 12 to 15 minutes at 180°C (350°F), turning halfway through the cooking time.

TIP
You can use a food processor to make breadcrumbs from stale bread or use crushed corn flakes. Serve the onion rings with the sauce of your choice.

FINGER FOOD

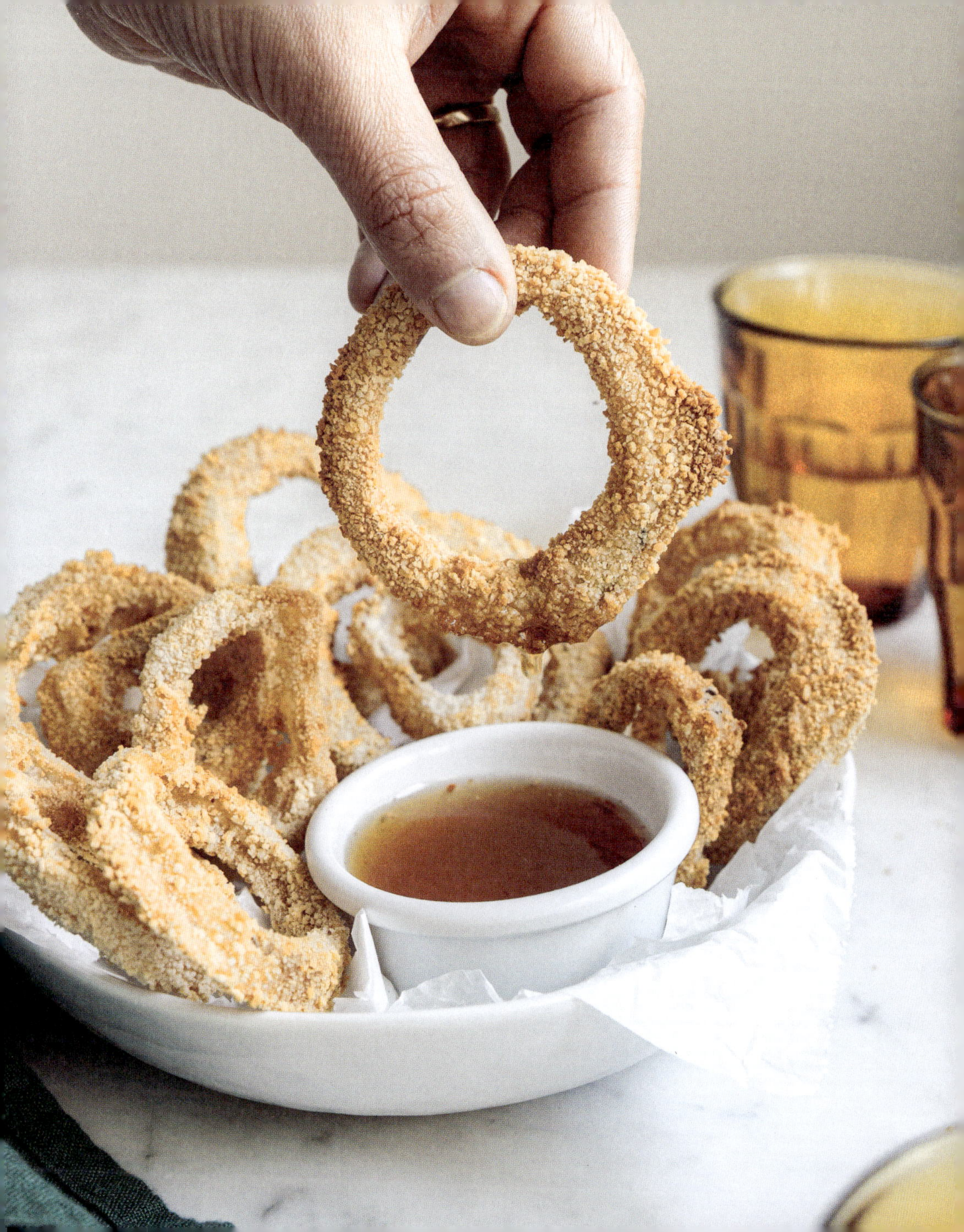

MAKES ABOUT 20 - MEDIUM - PREPARATION 20 MINUTES - COOKING 25 MINUTES

PUMPKIN BITES

- 350 g (12oz) pumpkin or squash, such as butternut or Kent
- 1 egg
- 100 g (3½ oz) plain (all-purpose) flour
- Pinch of spices of your choice, such as ground cumin or cinnamon, to taste
- Salt and black pepper
- Sunflower or vegetable oil, for brushing

1 Peel the pumpkin and cut it into small pieces. Cook in boiling water for 20 to 30 minutes until tender, or 10 to 12 minutes if using a steamer. You can also cook the pumpkin pieces in the air fryer for 10 to 15 minutes at 180°C (350°F).

2 Once the pumpkin is cooked, mash it up and mix in the egg as well as the flour, spices, salt and pepper.

3 Form small balls and lightly brush them with oil. Air fry for 8 minutes at 200°C (400°F).

TIP
For a more gourmet version, you can roll your pumpkin bites in breadcrumbs before cooking.

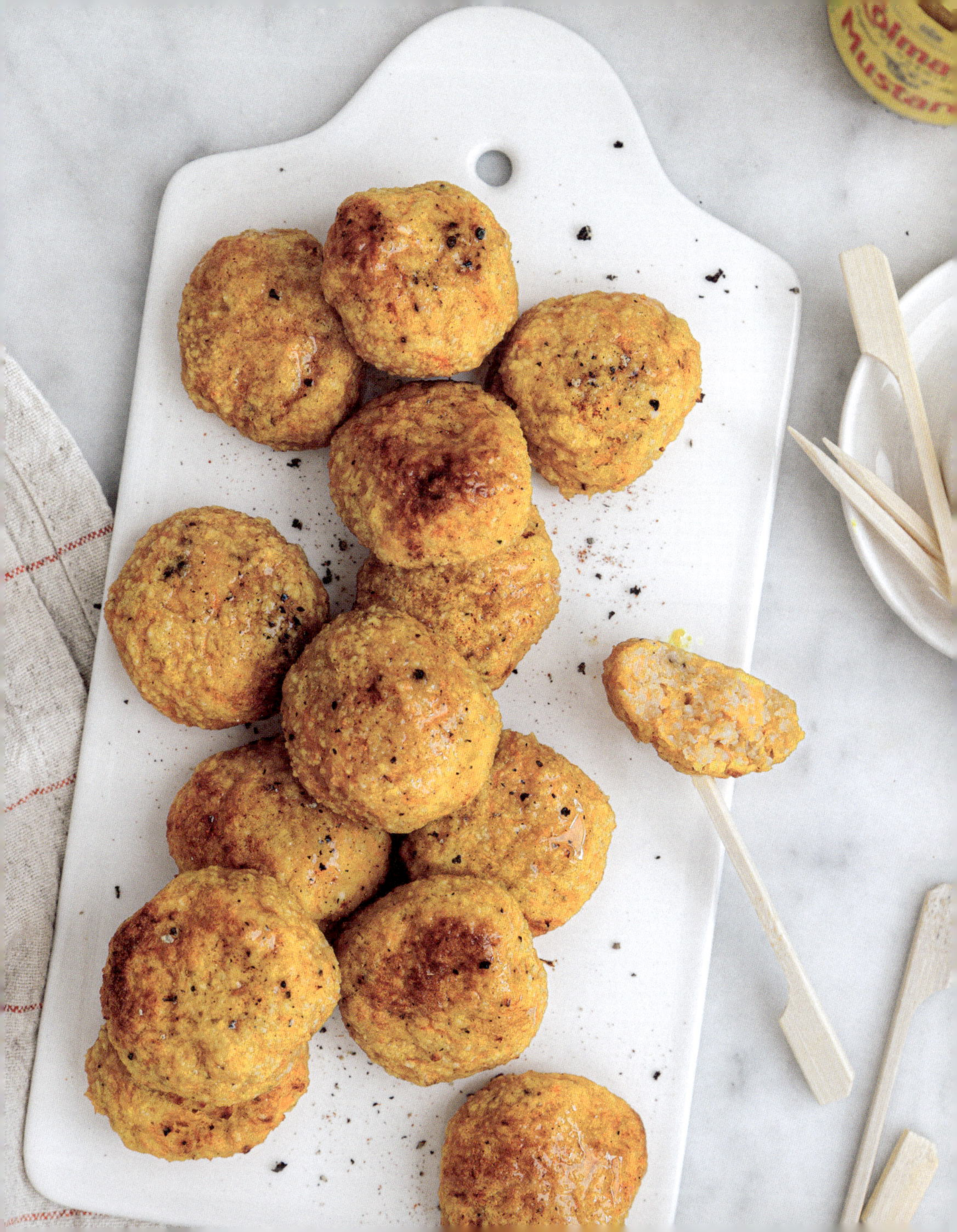

SERVES 2 - MEDIUM - PREPARATION 10 MINUTES - COOKING 9 MINUTES

MOZZA STICKS

- 1 mozzarella cheese block
- 2 eggs
- 100 g (3½ oz) plain (all-purpose) flour
- 100 g (3½ oz) breadcrumbs
- 1 teaspoon garlic powder
- 1 teaspoon paprika
- 1 teaspoon chilli powder

1 Cut the mozzarella into sticks about 5 mm–1 cm (¼–½ inch) wide. If you can't find mozzarella in a rectangular block, you can use the traditional ball shape. They don't have to be perfect 'stick' shapes.

2 In one bowl, whisk the eggs. Tip the flour into another bowl and in a third bowl, combine the breadcrumbs with the spices. Coat each stick first with flour, then dip in the egg and lastly roll in the breadcrumbs.

3 Place the sticks in the air fryer basket and cook for 9 minutes at 180°C (350°F), turning halfway through the cooking time. Serve with the sauce of your choice.

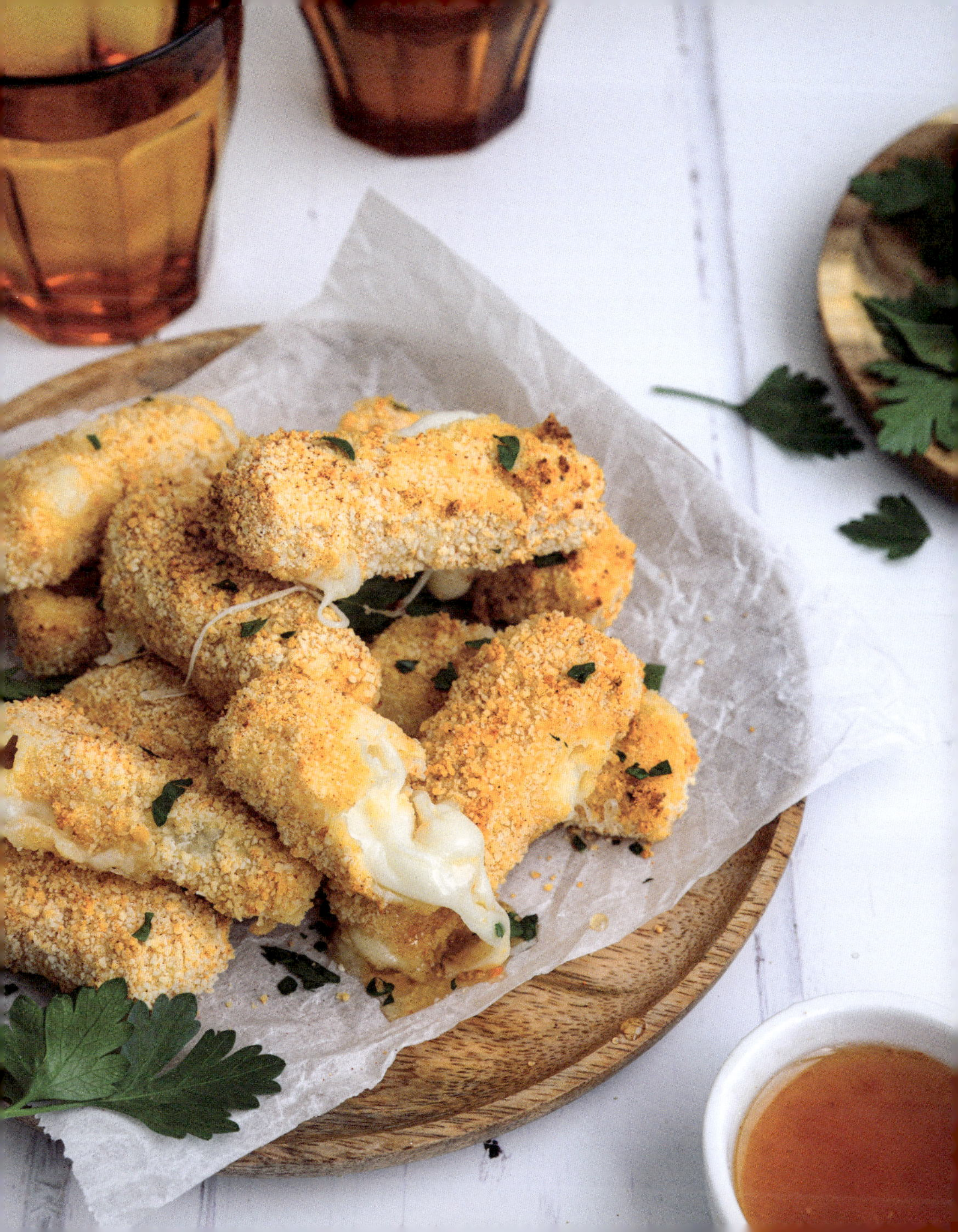

MAKES 8 - MEDIUM - PREPARATION 20 MINUTES - COOKING 10 MINUTES

TUNA TRIANGLES

- 150 g (5½ oz) tuna in spring water
- 80 g (2¾ oz) smooth, creamy ricotta
- 80 g (2¾ oz) cottage cheese
- 1 teaspoon chopped parsley
- Juice of 1 lemon
- 1–2 teaspoons spices or condiments, such as mustard, ketchup (tomato sauce) or curry powder
- Salt and black pepper
- 4 sheets brik or filo (phyllo) pastry
- Melted butter (optional)
- Sunflower or vegetable oil or 1 egg, for brushing
- Lemon wedges, to serve

1 In a bowl, combine the tuna with the ricotta and cottage cheese. Add the chopped parsley, lemon juice and spices and season with salt and pepper.

2 Cut the pastry sheets in half. If using brik pastry, fold the rounded edge over to the other edge to make a rectangle. If using filo pastry, brush with melted butter. Place a dollop of tuna filling at the bottom of each half. Fold the pastry over diagonally to form a triangle, then continue folding the parcel in a triangle shape to the end.

3 Brush with a little melted butter, oil or beaten egg and cook in the air fryer basket for 10 minutes at 180°C (350°F). Serve with lemon wedges.

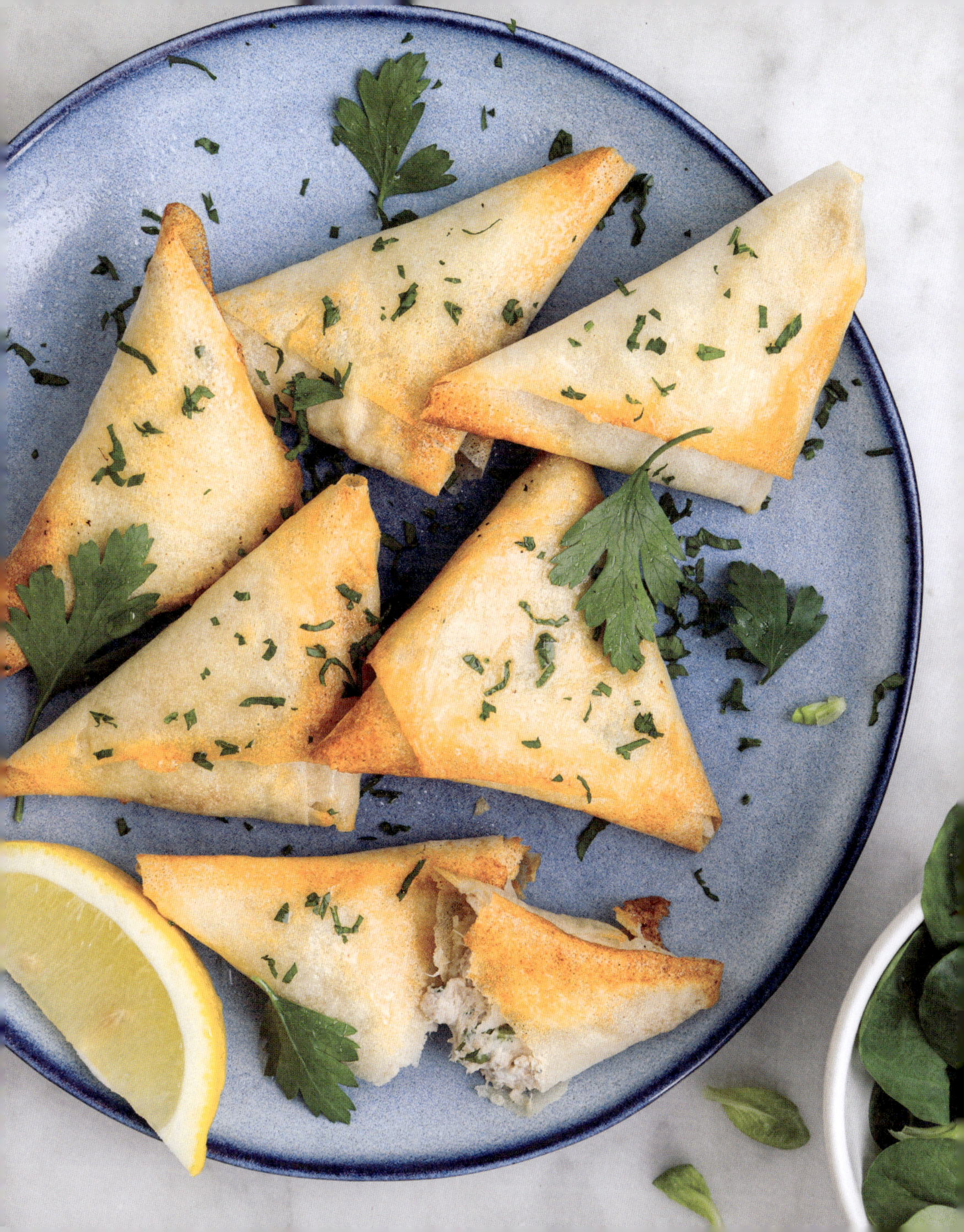

MAKES 4-6 - EASY - PREPARATION 10 MINUTES - COOKING 6 MINUTES

MINI PIZZA BAGUETTES

- 1 small baguette or 4-6 bread rolls
- 100 g (3½ oz) tomato paste (concentrated purée)
- 1 tablespoon herbes de Provence (mixed herbs)
- 2 large slices ham
- ½ onion, peeled and chopped
- 100 g (3½ oz) mushrooms, sliced
- 60 g (2¼ oz) shredded mozzarella cheese

1 Cut the bread in half and then slice open horizontally. Spread each piece with tomato paste. Sprinkle with herbes de Provence, then add pieces of ham, chopped onion and sliced mushrooms.

2 Sprinkle with the shredded mozzarella and cook in the air fryer for 6 minutes at 200°C (400°F). Fold the baguette back up to make sandwiches and cut each baguette half into two or three pieces.

TIP
This recipe works with any toppings! Try serving some raw vegetables with your finger food to make it healthier.

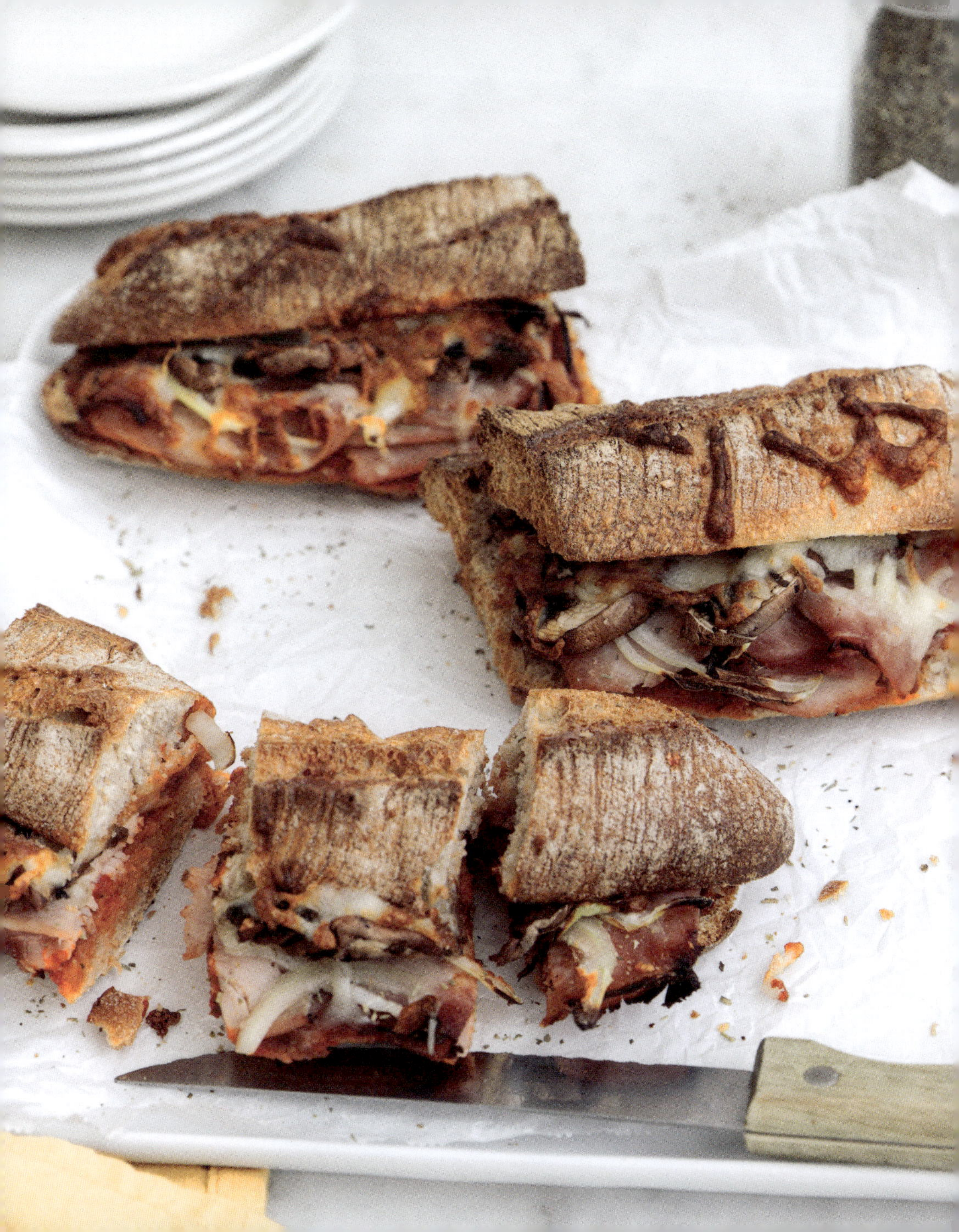

SERVES 2 - EASY - PREPARATION 5 MINUTES - COOKING 10 MINUTES

BAKED CAMEMBERT

- 1 Camembert cheese (in a wooden box)
- Fresh or dried thyme, to taste
- 1 teaspoon honey
- 60 g (2¼ oz) baguette or other bread, sliced

1 Remove the Camembert from its box and discard the rest of the packaging. Score the top of the Camembert in a grid pattern and return to the box.

2 Sprinkle with thyme and drizzle the honey on top.

3 Bake the Camembert for 10 minutes at 200°C (400°F) in the air fryer basket.

4 You can also air fry the slices of baguette with the cheese so that they become nice and crispy! Serve with the Camembert.

TIP
Baked Camembert is an irresistibly gooey pre-dinner treat!

FINGER FOOD

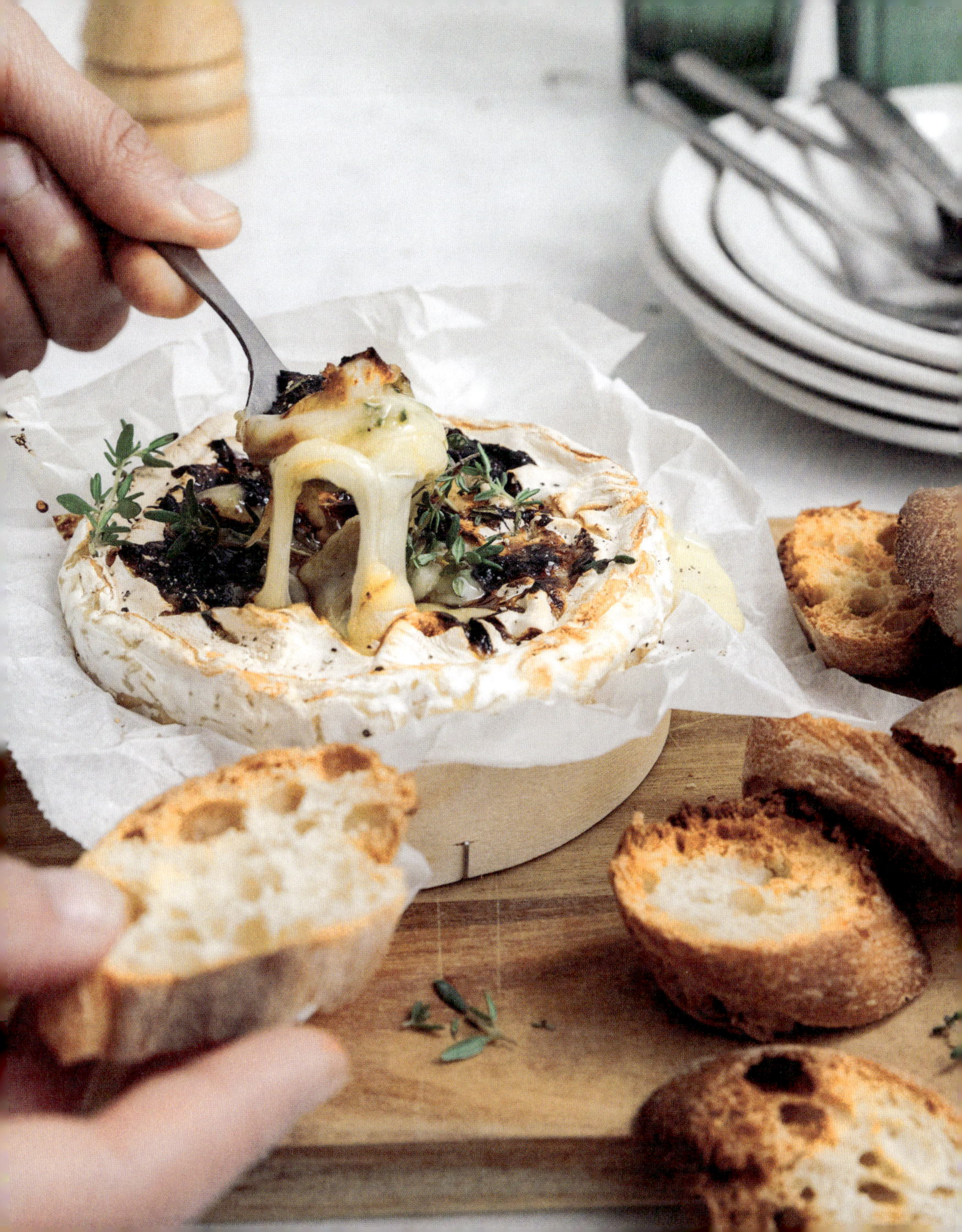

SERVES 2 - EASY - PREPARATION 10 MINUTES - COOKING 5 MINUTES

SALTED POPCORN

- 75 g (2½ oz) popcorn kernels
- 1 teaspoon sunflower or vegetable oil
- Paprika or other spices, to taste
- Sea salt
- Spray oil

1 Add the corn kernels, oil, spices and sea salt to a bowl and mix well.

2 Place a sheet of aluminium foil in the bottom of the air fryer basket and place the kernels on top. Spray with a little oil.

3 Bake for 5 minutes at 200°C (400°F).

TIP
You can add any spices you like and you can also make a sweet version of this recipe.

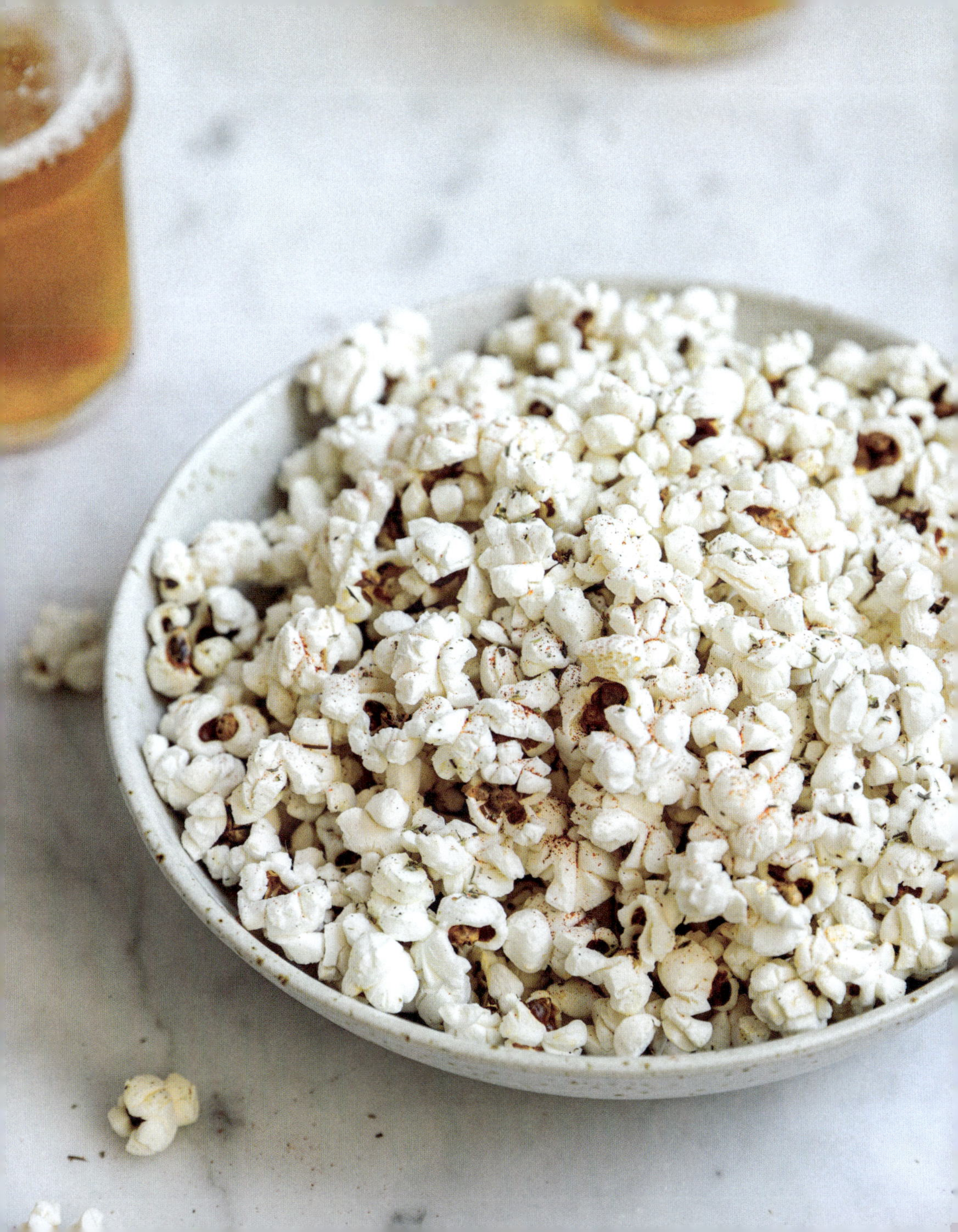

MAKES 8 - MEDIUM - PREPARATION 20 MINUTES - COOKING 10 MINUTES

VEGETABLE SPRING ROLLS

- ½ carrot
- ½ courgette (zucchini)
- Spray oil
- 1 egg, beaten
- Salt and black pepper
- 4 sheets brik or spring roll pastry
- 20 g (¾ oz) goat's cheese
- Sunflower or vegetable oil or 1 egg, for brushing

1 Peel the carrot, then grate the courgette and carrot. Fry in a lightly oiled pan for a few minutes. Add the beaten egg to the vegetables and mix until the egg is cooked. Season with salt and pepper.

2 Cut the pastry sheets in half and add a spoonful of the vegetable and egg mixture to the bottom of the sheet. Add crumbled goat's cheese on top of the filling. Fold in the sides, then start rolling the pastry over the filling to form a cigar shape. Continue folding the pastry to the end.

3 Brush with a little oil or beaten egg. Cook in the air fryer for 10 minutes at 180°C (350°F).

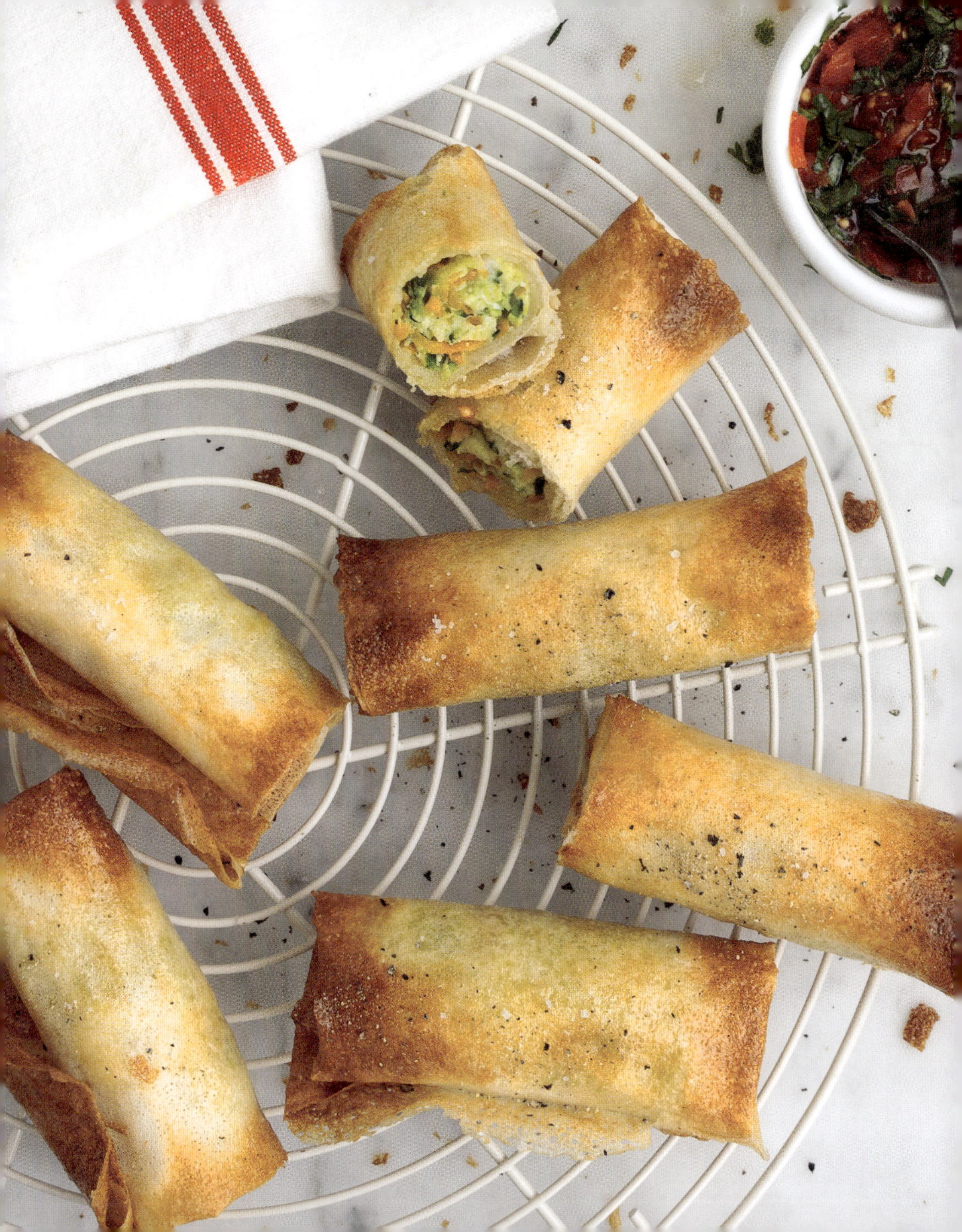

LUNCH & DINNER

Croque madame	62	Mini ham croissants	86
Fish & crisps	64	Veggie lasagne	88
Jacket potatoes	66	Bruschetta	90
Roasted broccoli	68	Crumbed egg yolks	92
Chicken nuggets	70	Meatballs & potato rosti	94
Cheeseburgers	72	Stuffed tomatoes	96
Creamy tomato and ham pasta	74	Roasted carrots	98
		Spicy chicken skewers	100
Pistachio-crusted salmon	76	Beef samosas	102
Savoury loaf	78	Baked cod	104
Chicken fajitas	80	Roasted vegetable fries	106
Smashed butternut	82	Frittata with red pepper	108
Cordon bleu	84	Roasted summer vegetables	110

SERVES 2 - EASY - PREPARATION 10 MINUTES - COOKING 10 MINUTES

CROQUE MADAME

- 1 tablespoon sour cream
- 1 tablespoon smooth, creamy ricotta
- Salt and black pepper
- Grated nutmeg, to taste
- 4 slices wholemeal bread
- 2 slices ham
- 60 g (2¼ oz) Gruyère or Jarlsberg cheese, grated
- 2 fried eggs

1 In a bowl, mix the sour cream and ricotta with a little salt, pepper and nutmeg.

2 Assemble the sandwiches: spread a little cream/ricotta mixture on two slices of bread, then add a slice of ham on each and a little grated cheese and top with the other two slices of bread. Cover this second slice of bread with the remaining cream/ricotta mixture and sprinkle with more grated cheese.

3 Cook in the air fryer basket at 200°C (400°F) for 10 minutes. Serve with a fried egg on top.

TIP
Serve this sandwich with a nice leafy salad. You can also make a croque monsieur by simply leaving out the fried egg on top of the sandwich.

LUNCH & DINNER

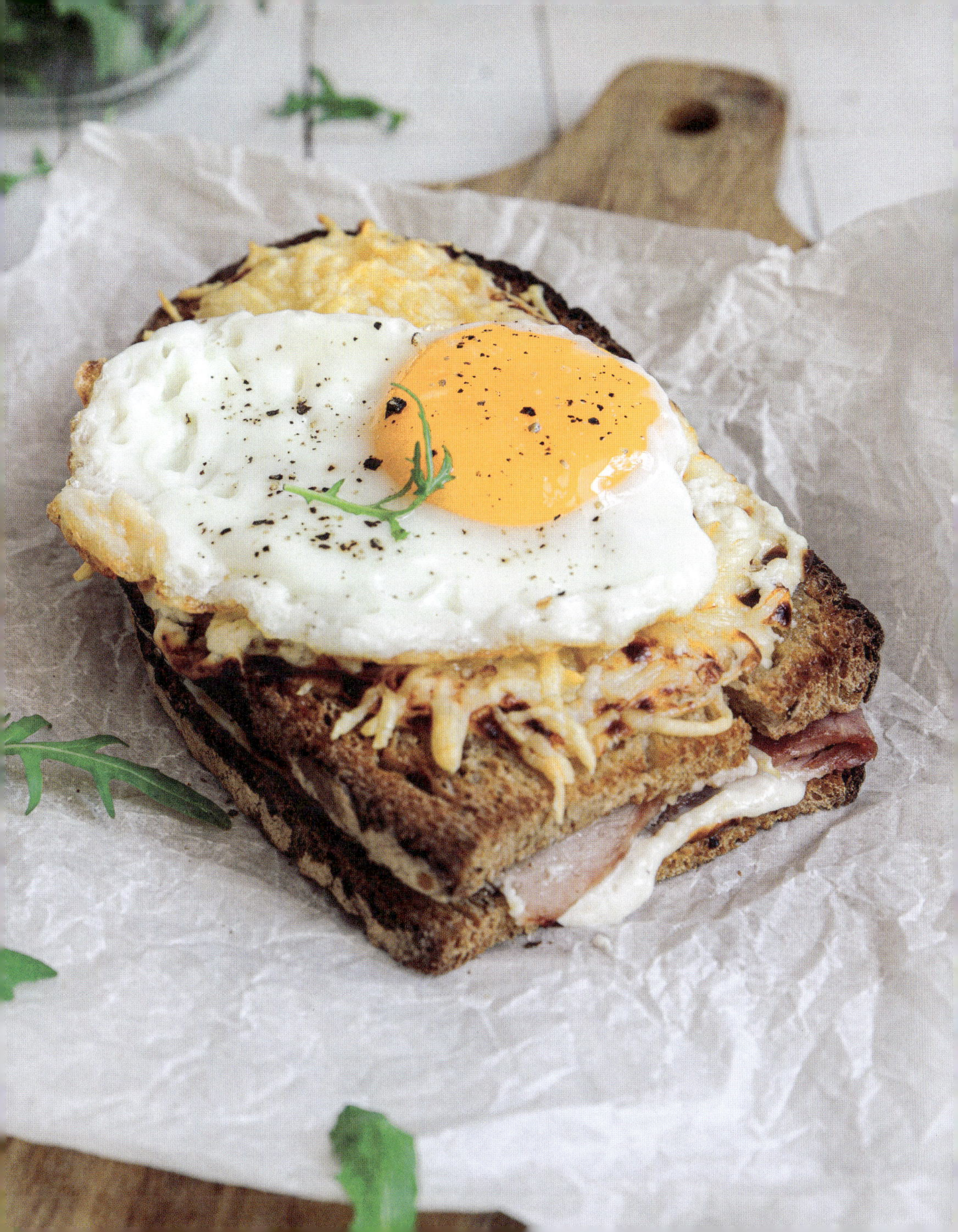

SERVES 2 - MEDIUM - PREPARATION 15 MINUTES - COOKING 15 MINUTES

FISH & CRISPS

- 60 g (2¼ oz) plain (all-purpose) flour, plus extra for flouring
- 1 teaspoon baking powder
- 1 teaspoon paprika
- 1 teaspoon chilli powder
- Salt and black pepper
- 250 ml (9fl oz) blonde or pilsner beer
- 300 g (10½ oz) white fish fillets, such as cod or hoki, chopped into large chunks
- Lemon wedges, to serve
- Potato crisps, to serve (see recipe on page 38 for homemade)

1 In a bowl, combine the flour, baking powder, spices, salt and pepper. Gently and gradually pour the beer into the dry ingredients and mix well to avoid lumps. The batter should be smooth.

2 Put some extra flour on a plate. Coat each fish fillet with the flour first, then coat well with the beer batter.

3 Place the coated fish fillets in the air fryer basket and cook for 15 minutes at 180°C (350°F), turning halfway through the cooking time. Serve with lemon wedges and potato crisps.

TIP
For a lighter version, you can replace the beer with sparkling water.

LUNCH & DINNER

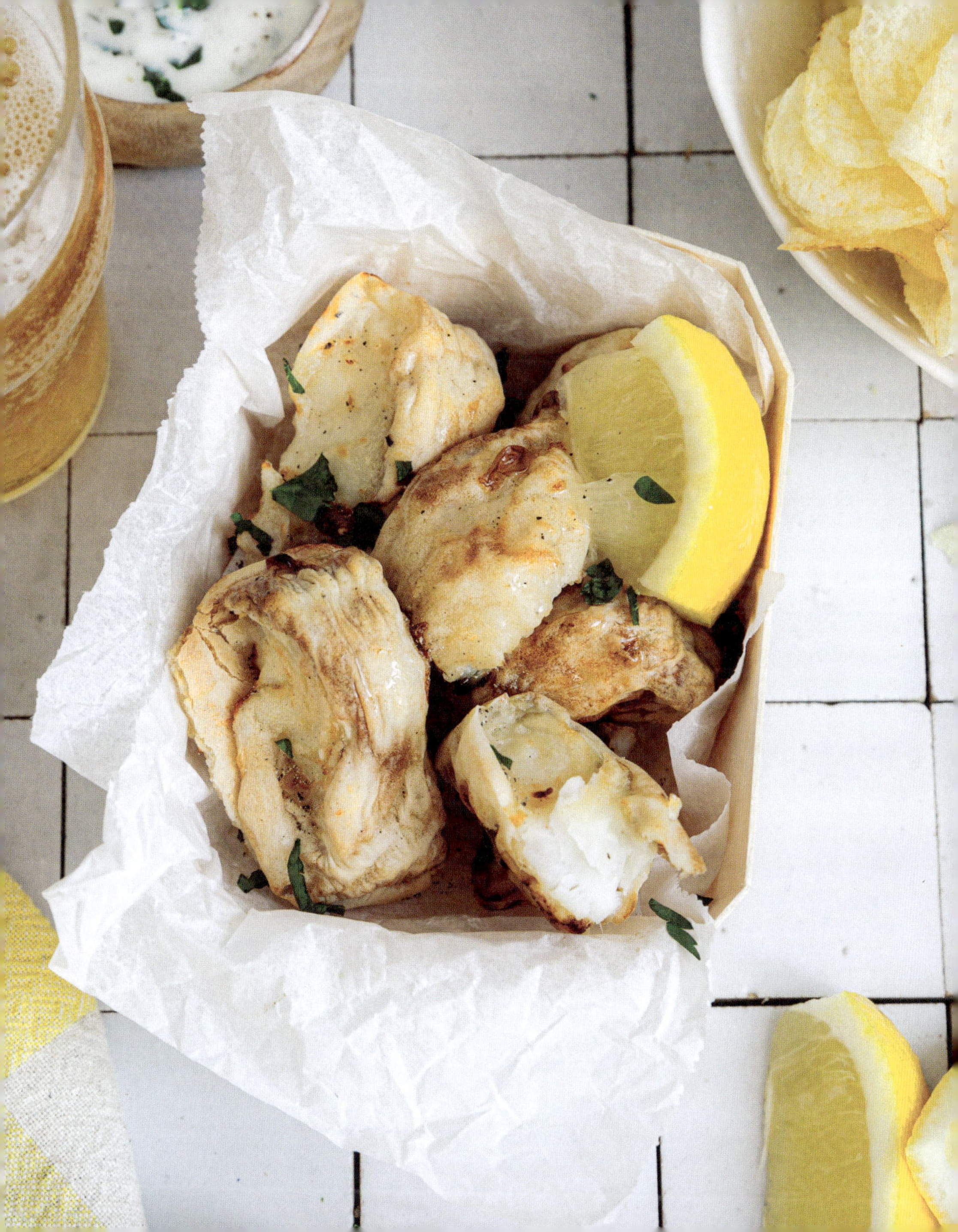

SERVES 2 - MEDIUM - PREPARATION 15 MINUTES - COOKING 35 MINUTES

JACKET POTATOES

- 2 teaspoons ground cumin
- 2 teaspoons ground turmeric
- 2 teaspoons paprika
- 2 teaspoons chilli powder
- Salt and black pepper
- 2 baking potatoes
- 1 tablespoon sunflower or vegetable oil
- 1 onion, peeled and chopped
- ½ green pepper (capsicum), seeds and core removed, chopped
- 150 g (5½ oz) beef mince
- 2 eggs, beaten
- 200 g (7 oz) tomato passata (puréed tomatoes)
- 60 g (2¼ oz) Gruyère or mozzarella cheese, grated

1 Mix together the spices and some salt and pepper. In a bowl, coat the whole unpeeled potatoes with oil and half the spice mix, then air fry for 25 to 30 minutes at 190°C (375°F).

2 While the potatoes are cooking, make the filling. In a lightly oiled frying pan, brown the chopped onion and green pepper with the beef mince over a medium heat for 5 to 10 minutes, until the vegetables start to colour and the beef mince browns. Add the remaining spice mix and the beaten eggs and stir until the eggs are cooked. Add the tomato passata and cook for a further couple of minutes. (You can leave the filling mixture covered over a gentle heat until the potatoes are cooked.)

3 Once the potatoes are cooked, cut them in half without going all the way through and top them with the meat mixture. Sprinkle with grated Gruyère or mozzarella cheese and bake again for 5 minutes at 200°C (400°F) in the air fryer basket.

TIP
You can also make this recipe with a sweet potato. For a vegetarian version, simply replace the meat with plant-based mince.

LUNCH & DINNER

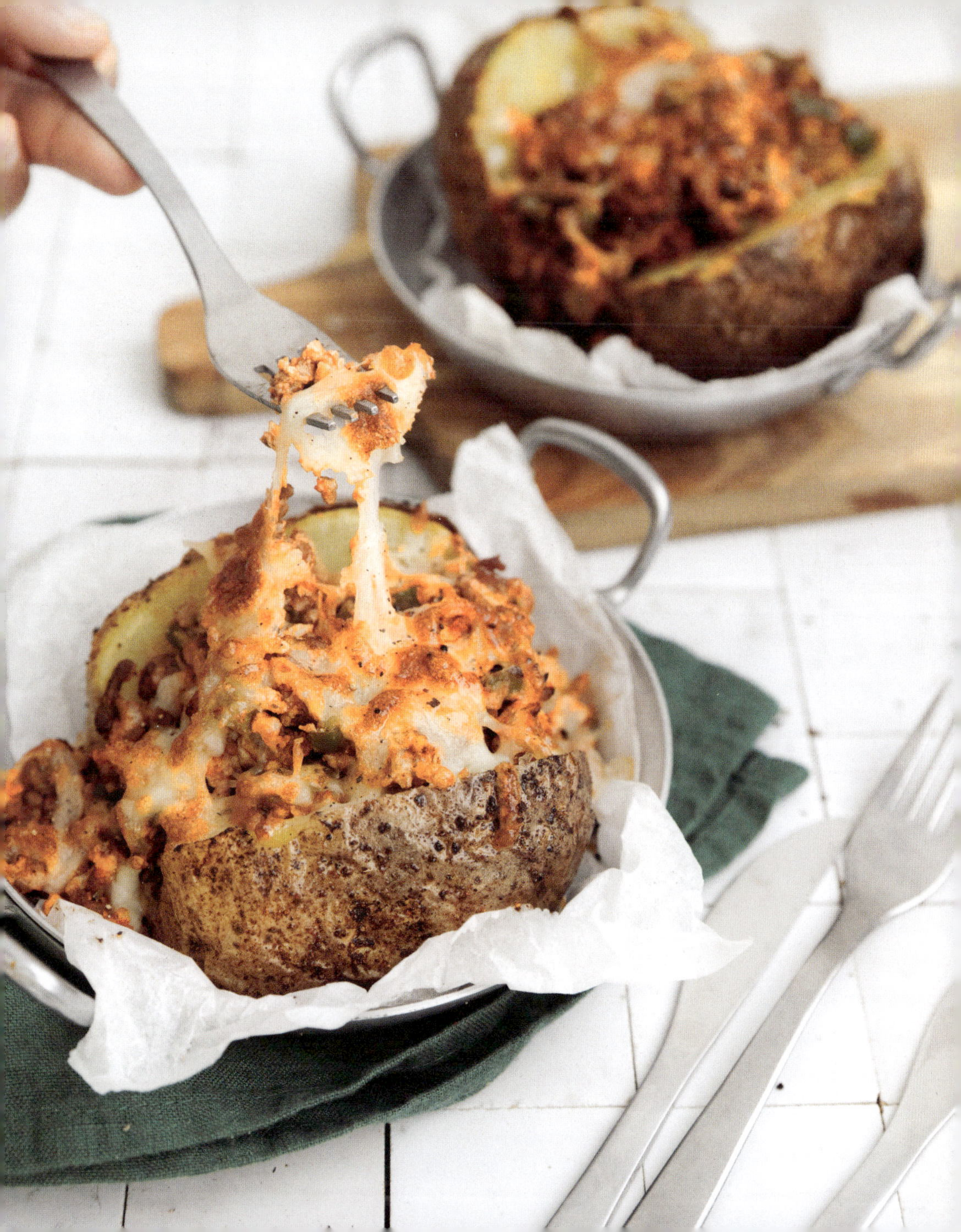

SERVES 2 - MEDIUM - PREPARATION 10 MINUTES - COOKING 20 MINUTES

ROASTED BROCCOLI

- 1 egg, beaten
- 20 g (¾ oz) plain (all purpose) flour
- 1 tablespoon spice of your choice, such as curry powder or paprika
- Salt
- 20 g (¾ oz) breadcrumbs
- 20 g (¾ oz) Parmesan cheese, grated
- Olive oil
- ½ broccoli head, cut into florets
- Sauces of your choice, such as ketchup, mustard or mayonnaise, to serve

1 In a bowl, mix together the beaten egg, flour, spices and salt. In another bowl, combine the breadcrumbs, Parmesan and a drizzle of olive oil.

2 Dip the broccoli florets into the egg batter and then into the Parmesan and breadcrumbs mixture.

3 Bake in the air fryer basket for 20 minutes at 180°C (350°F), turning halfway through the cooking time. Serve with condiments of your choice.

TIP
You can easily replace the broccoli with cauliflower in this recipe.

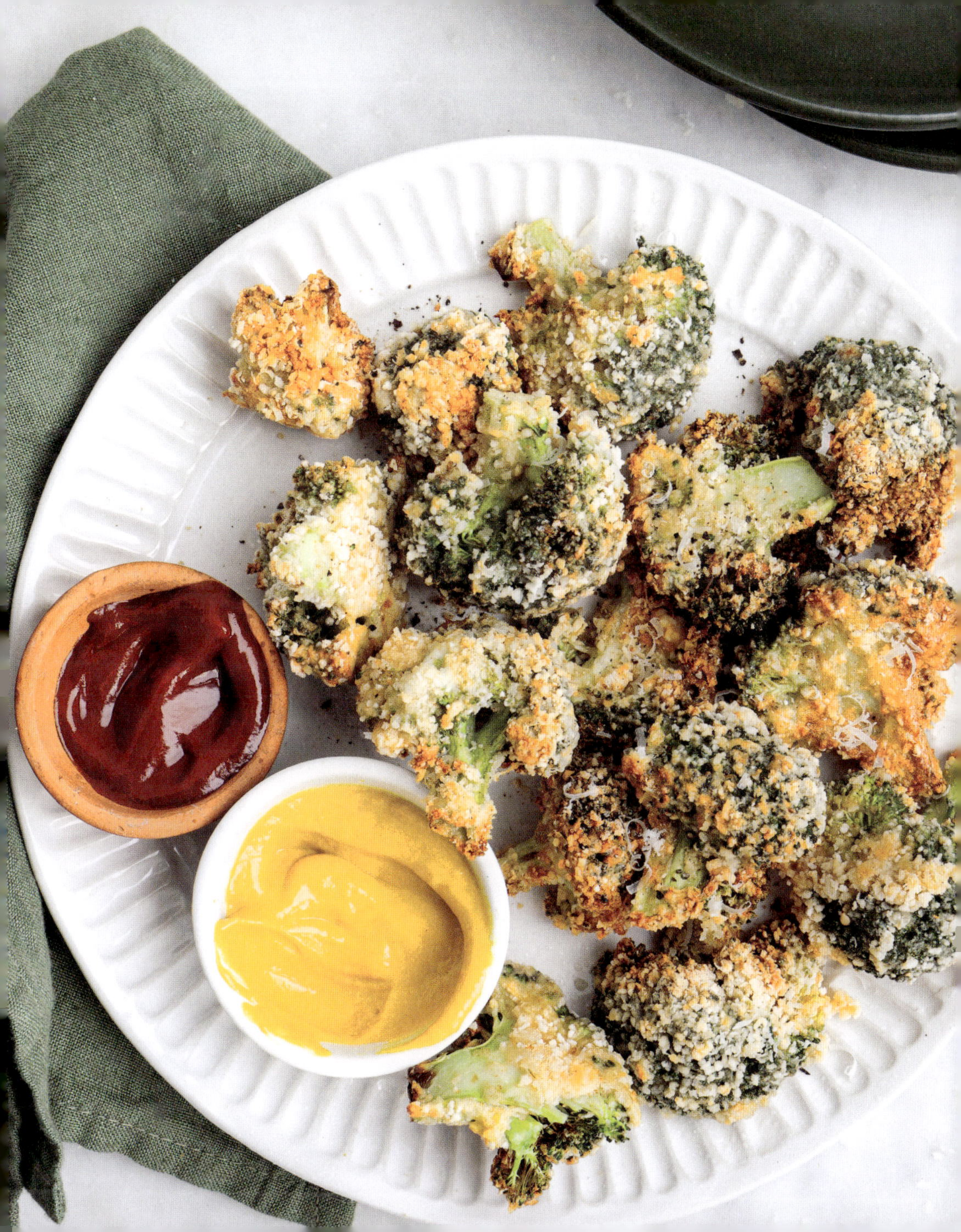

SERVES 2 - ADVANCED - PREPARATION 20 MINUTES - COOKING 15 MINUTES

CHICKEN NUGGETS

- 250 g (9 oz) chicken breast, roughly chopped
- 1 egg (white and yolk separated)
- 50 g (1¾ oz) plain (all-purpose) flour
- Spices, such as garlic powder, paprika and chilli, to taste
- Salt and black pepper
- 30 ml (1 fl oz) milk
- 50 g (1¾ oz) breadcrumbs

1 Put the chicken and egg white in a blender and blend to form a paste.

2 In one bowl, combine the flour with the spices and some salt and pepper. In another bowl, mix the beaten egg yolk with the milk. Put the breadcrumbs in a third bowl.

3 Form balls in the shape of nuggets with the chicken paste and then dip the nuggets in the flour, then the egg, and lastly the breadcrumbs. You can double-crumb the nuggets by repeating the process.

4 Place the nuggets in the air fryer basket and bake for 15 minutes at 190°C (375°F). Turn the nuggets after 10 minutes.

TIP
Enjoy these nuggets with a serve of steamed vegetables and a dip of your choice.

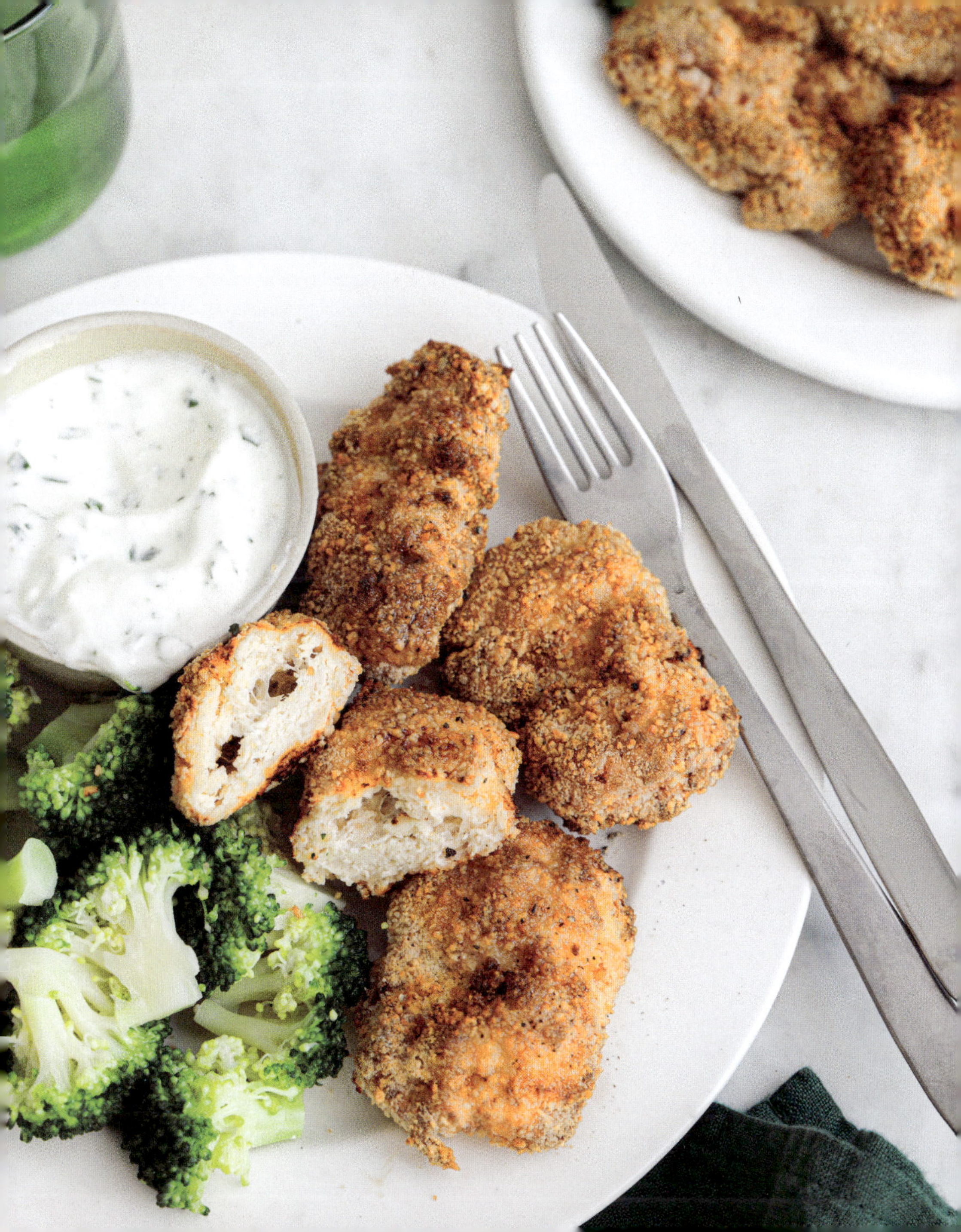

SERVES 2 - MEDIUM - PREPARATION 20 MINUTES - COOKING 10 MINUTES

CHEESEBURGERS

- 2 lean beef burger patties
- 1 red onion, peeled and cut into rings
- 2 slices cheese of your choice
- 2 burger buns
- Sauce of your choice, such as ketchup, mustard or mayonnaise
- Few lettuce leaves
- 1 tomato, sliced

1. Place the burger patties in the air fryer basket with the sliced onion and cook for 10 minutes at 180°C (350°F). For the last 2 minutes of cooking, turn the patties over and add a slice of cheese on top.

2. If there's space, put the burger buns in the basket next to the patties when you add the cheese.

3. Assemble the burgers by spreading your condiment of choice on the bottom half of the buns. Add the lettuce, beef patty, cheese, onion and tomato and top with the other bun half.

TIP
For a veggie burger, you can use a vegetable patty.

LUNCH & DINNER

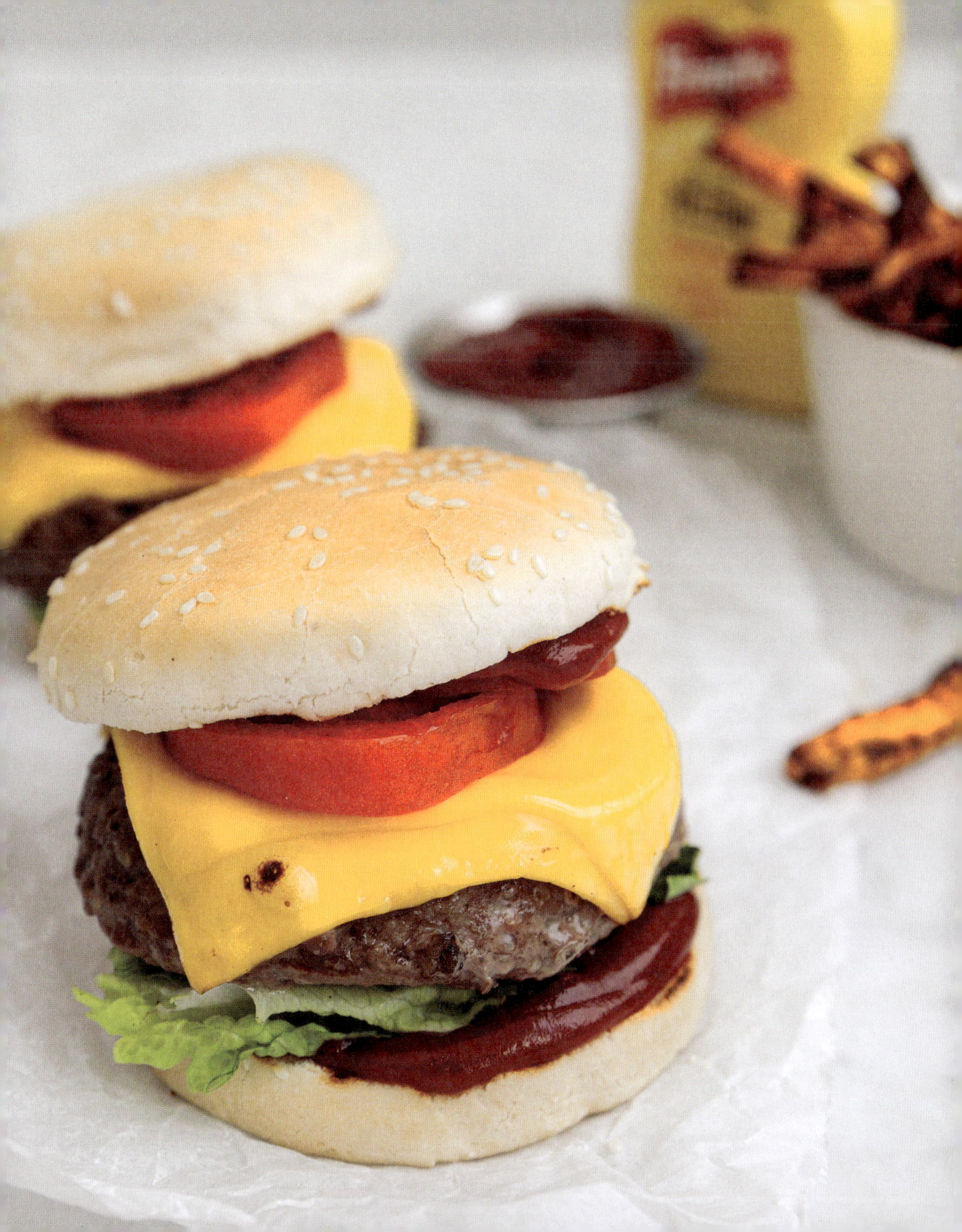

SERVES 2 - EASY - PREPARATION 10 MINUTES - COOKING 15 MINUTES

CREAMY TOMATO AND HAM PASTA

- 100 g (3½ oz) garlic and herb soft cream cheese
- 100 g (3½ oz) cherry tomatoes, larger ones halved
- 150 g (5½ oz) red pepper (capsicum), seeds and core removed, sliced
- Olive oil
- 2 tablespoons Italian herb mix
- Fresh or dried thyme, to taste
- Fresh or dried rosemary, to taste
- 100 g (3½ oz) dried pasta
- 2 slices ham, chopped
- 1–2 tablespoons smooth, creamy ricotta or sour cream (optional)

1 Place the soft cream cheese in the centre of the air fryer pan and arrange the cherry tomatoes and pepper around the cheese.

2 Add a drizzle of olive oil and the herbs and air fry for 15 minutes at 200°C (400°F).

3 Meanwhile, cook the pasta in a saucepan of salted boiling water according to the packet instructions. Once cooked, drain the pasta and return to the saucepan.

4 Add the cooked vegetables and chopped ham to the pasta and mix well. Add 1 or 2 tablespoons of ricotta or sour cream for a creamier finish.

TIP
You can vary the vegetables and cheese to your taste. For a veggie version, remove the ham.

LUNCH & DINNER

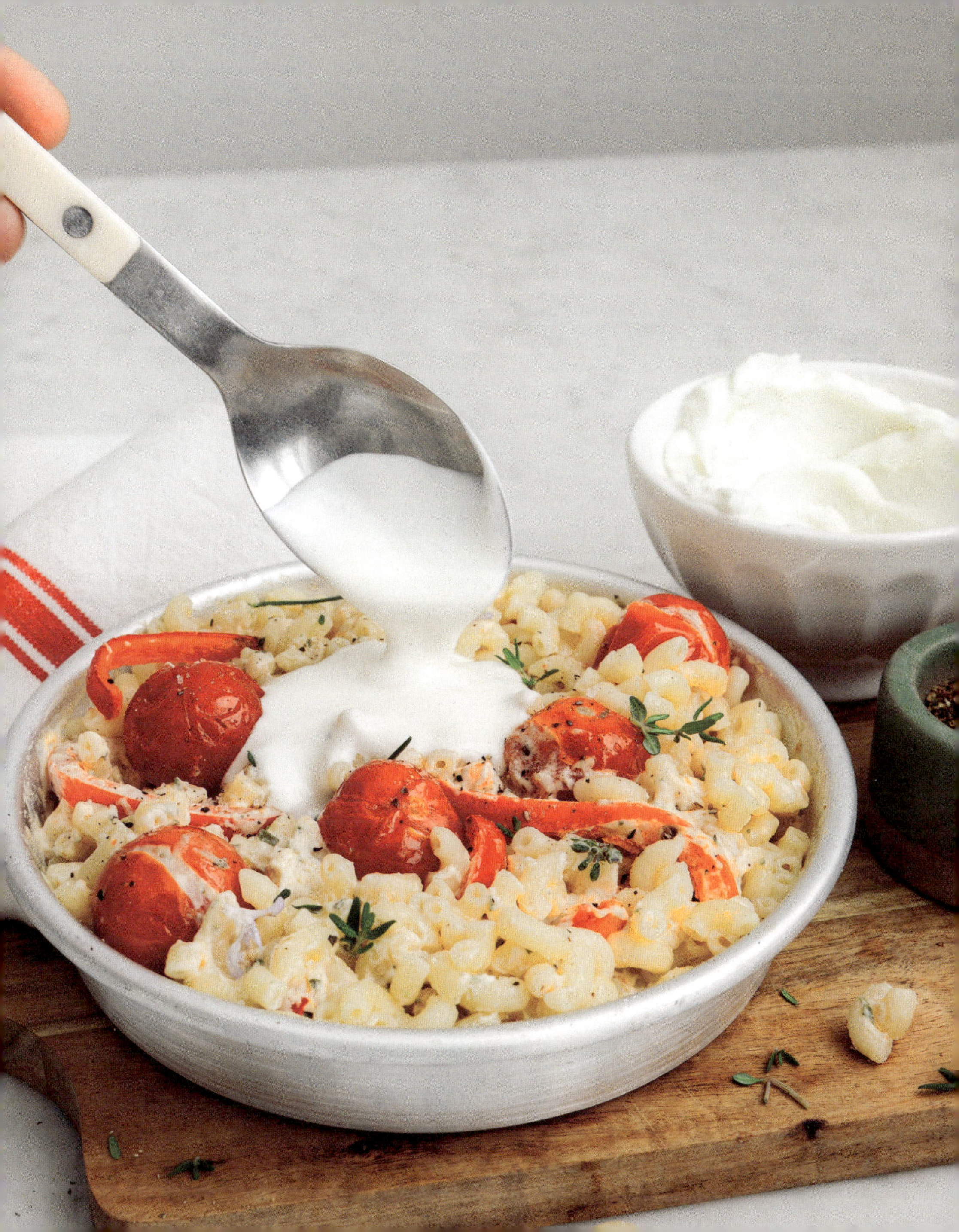

SERVES 2 - EASY - PREPARATION 15 MINUTES - COOKING 11 MINUTES

PISTACHIO-CRUSTED SALMON

- 2 salmon portions
- 1 teaspoon honey
- Juice of 1 lemon
- 1 teaspoon Dijon mustard
- 1 teaspoon garlic powder
- 40 g (1½ oz) pistachios, finely chopped
- Salt and black pepper

1. Pat the salmon portions dry using paper towels and place them in the air fryer basket. Bake for 6 minutes at 190°C (375°F).

2. In a bowl, combine the honey, lemon juice, mustard, garlic powder and chopped pistachios. Season with salt and pepper.

3. Once the salmon is cooked, spread the mixture on top of the portions and cook for a further 5 minutes in the air fryer.

TIP

Include a serving of carbohydrates and vegetables to create a well-rounded and nutritious meal.

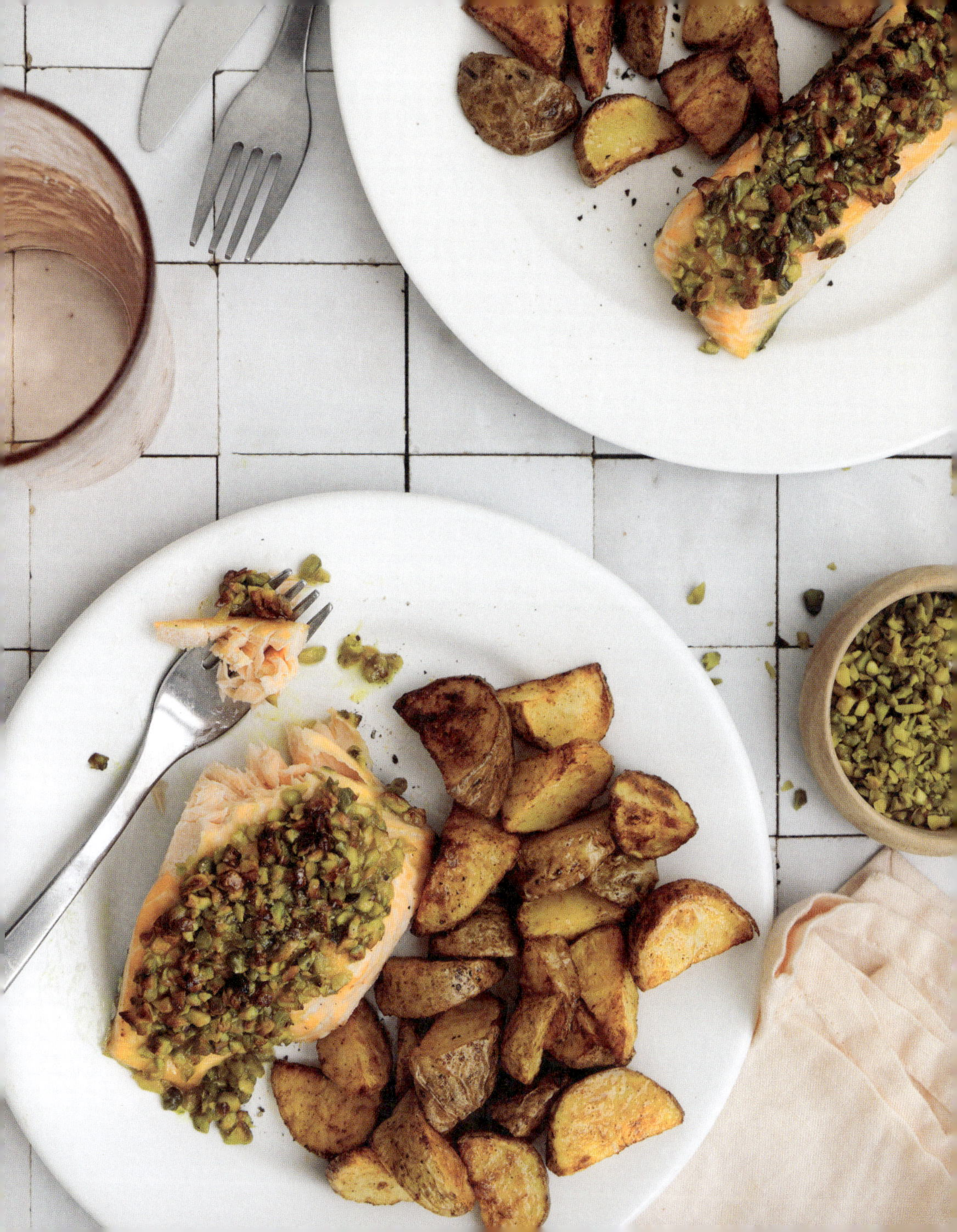

SERVES 2 - EASY - PREPARATION 10 MINUTES - COOKING 40 MINUTES

SAVOURY LOAF

- 120 g (4¼ oz) plain (all-purpose) flour
- 1 teaspoon baking powder
- Fresh or dried basil, to taste
- Salt and black pepper
- 2 eggs
- 25 ml (1 fl oz) double (heavy) cream
- 25 g (1 oz) cottage cheese
- Few pitted olives
- 60 g (2¼ oz) Gruyère or Jarlsberg cheese, grated
- 130 g (4½ oz) ham, chopped

1. In a bowl, combine the flour, baking powder, basil, salt and pepper. Add the eggs, cream and cottage cheese and beat together. Add the olives, grated Gruyère and chopped ham and mix well.

2. Pour the batter into a greased air fryer-safe loaf tin and bake in the air fryer for 40 minutes at 170°C (350°F).

TIP
You can also use this batter to make muffins. For a veggie version, remove the ham and add feta cheese instead.

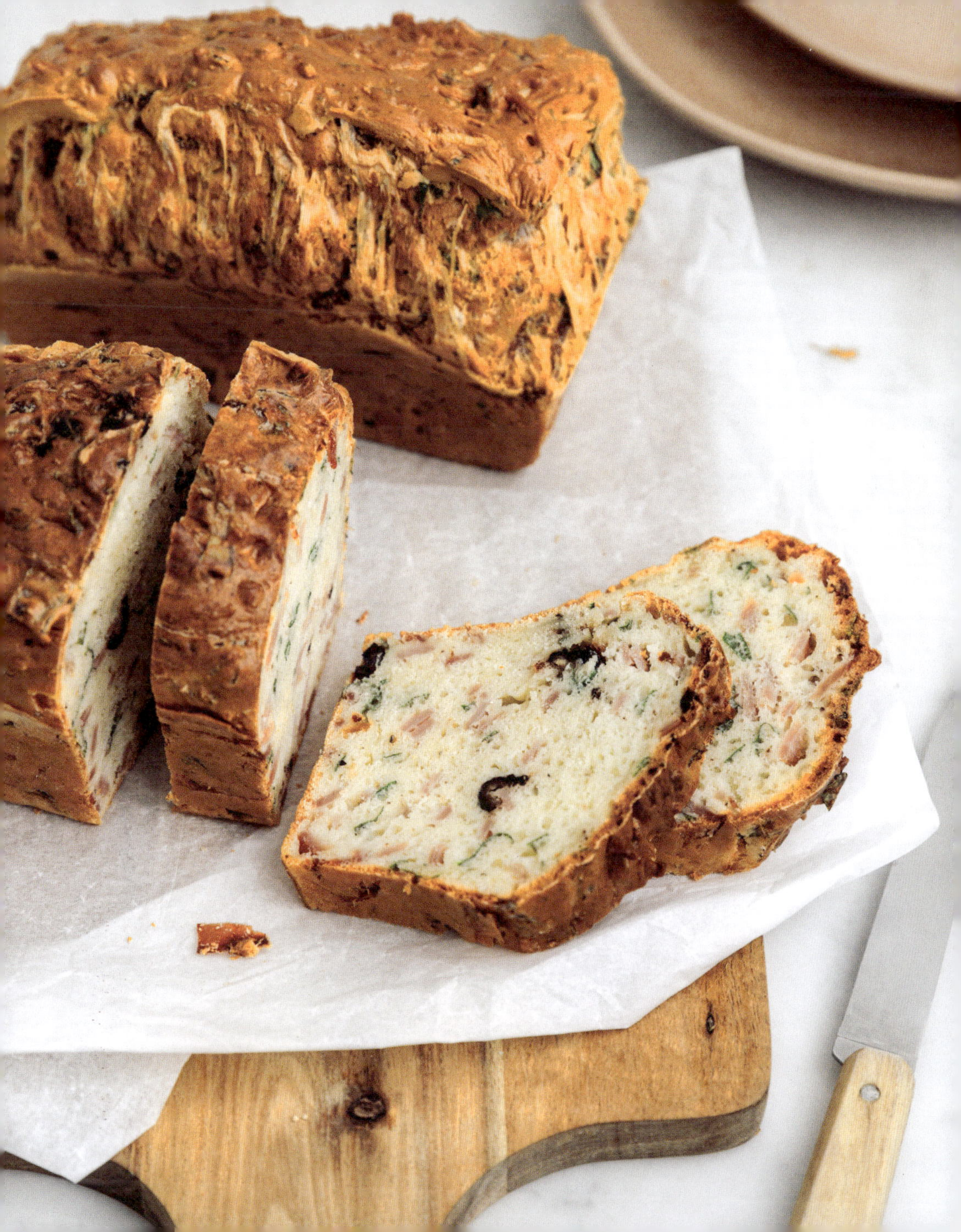

SERVES 2 - EASY - PREPARATION 15 MINUTES - COOKING 12 MINUTES

CHICKEN FAJITAS

- 250 g (9 oz) chicken breast
- 1 small onion, peeled and diced
- ½ red pepper (capsicum), seeds and core removed, diced
- ½ green pepper (capsicum), seeds and core removed, diced
- ½ yellow pepper (capsicum), seeds and core removed, diced
- Olive oil
- Pinch of ground cumin
- Pinch of ground turmeric
- Pinch of paprika
- Salt and black pepper
- 300 g (10½ oz) finely chopped tomatoes or tomato passata (puréed tomatoes)
- 2 large tortillas
- Lime wedges, to serve

1. Cut the chicken into small cubes and place in the air fryer basket with the diced onion and peppers. Add a drizzle of olive oil as well as the spices, salt and pepper. Mix well.

2. Cook for 12 minutes at 200°C (400°F), stirring halfway through the cooking time. Stir the chopped tomatoes or passata through the chicken and vegetables, then spoon the mixture into hot tortillas and serve with lime wedges.

TIP
You can serve these fajitas with a tasty homemade guacamole.

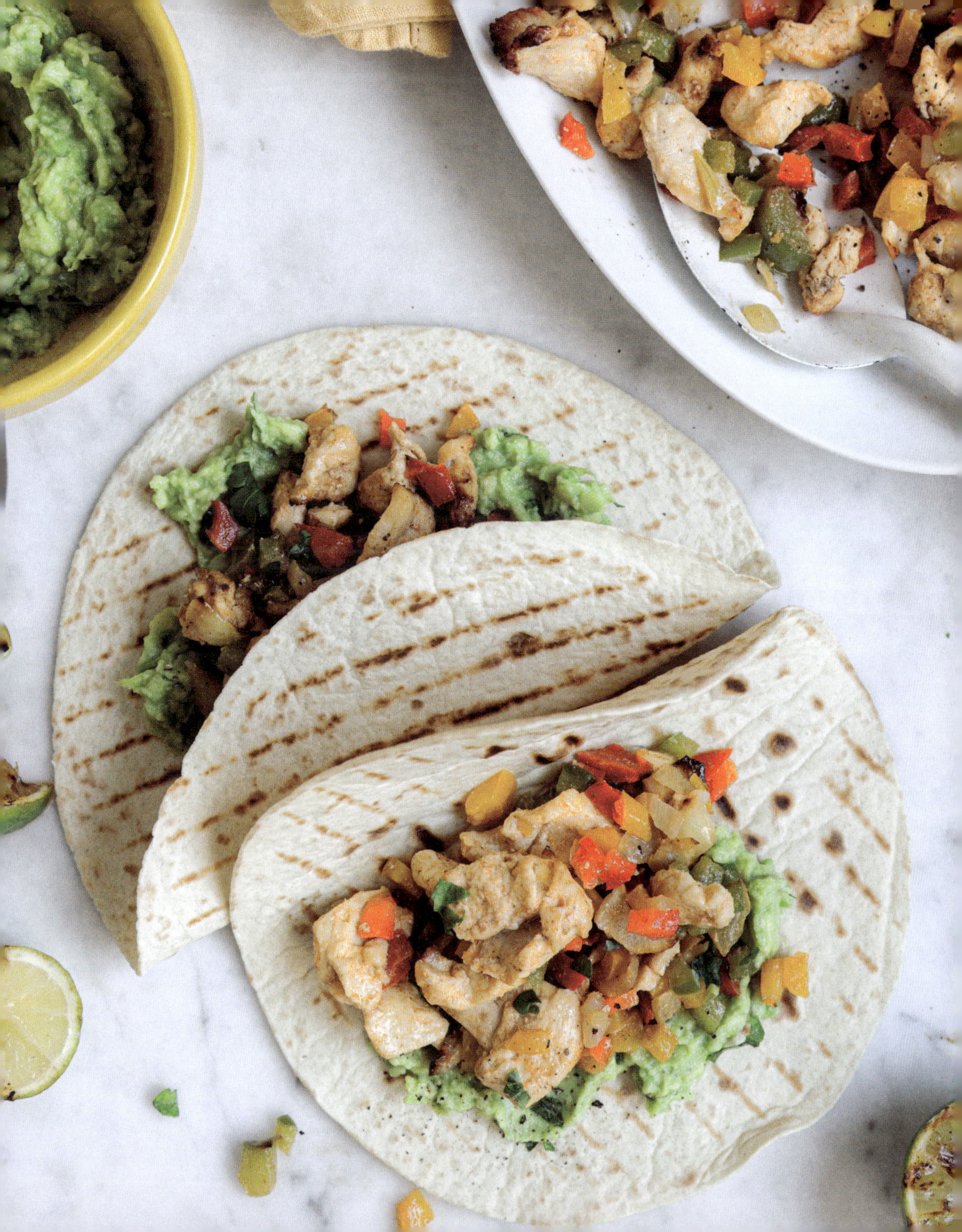

SERVES 2 - EASY - PREPARATION 20 MINUTES - COOKING 35 MINUTES

SMASHED BUTTERNUT

- 400 g (14 oz) butternut squash or pumpkin, peeled
- Salt
- 20 g (¾ oz) salted butter, chopped
- 1 teaspoon honey
- Fresh or dried thyme, to taste

1 Cut the peeled butternut or pumpkin into medium-sized pieces and cook in a saucepan of salted boiling water for 15 minutes.

2 Once cooked, place the butternut pieces in the air fryer basket and crush them with the back of a fork so you can see the fork marks. Add the chopped butter, honey and thyme on top of the butternut.

3 Bake in the air fryer basket for 20 minutes at 190°C (375°F).

TIP
This smashed butternut can be used in place of a hamburger bun if you or your guests are gluten free.

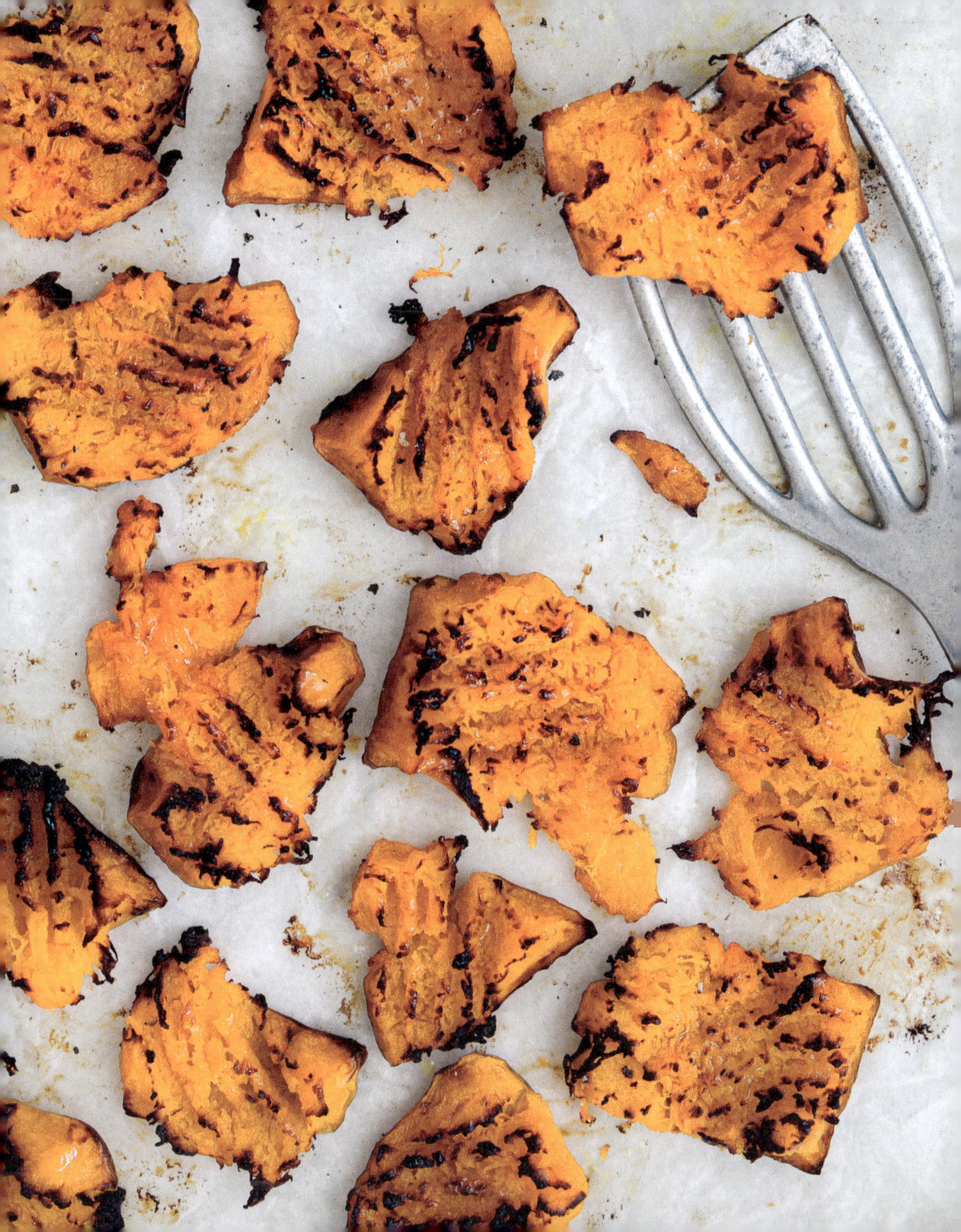

SERVES 2 - ADVANCED - PREPARATION 20 MINUTES - COOKING 15 MINUTES

CORDON BLEU

- 2 chicken breasts
- 2 slices Swiss cheese
- 2 slices ham
- 20 g (¾ oz) plain (all-purpose) flour
- 1 egg, beaten
- 40 g (1½ oz) breadcrumbs
- Spray oil
- Salt and black pepper

1 Bufferfly the chicken breasts in half lengthways and flatten them (you can use a rolling pin to pound them).

2 Place a slice of cheese and a slice of ham inside each breast. Fold the chicken breast in half again and press firmly on the edges to seal (use the rolling pin again if needed).

3 Tip the flour into a shallow bowl. Put the beaten egg in another bowl, and prepare a third bowl with the breadcrumbs. Dip the chicken breasts into the flour, then the egg, then the breadcrumbs, then repeat a second time.

4 Spray the air fryer basket with oil. Place the cordons bleus in the basket and cook for 15 minutes at 200°C (400°F), turning halfway through the cooking time. Check the chicken is cooked through before serving.

TIP
Serve these cordons bleus with a side of vegetables, such as steamed green beans.

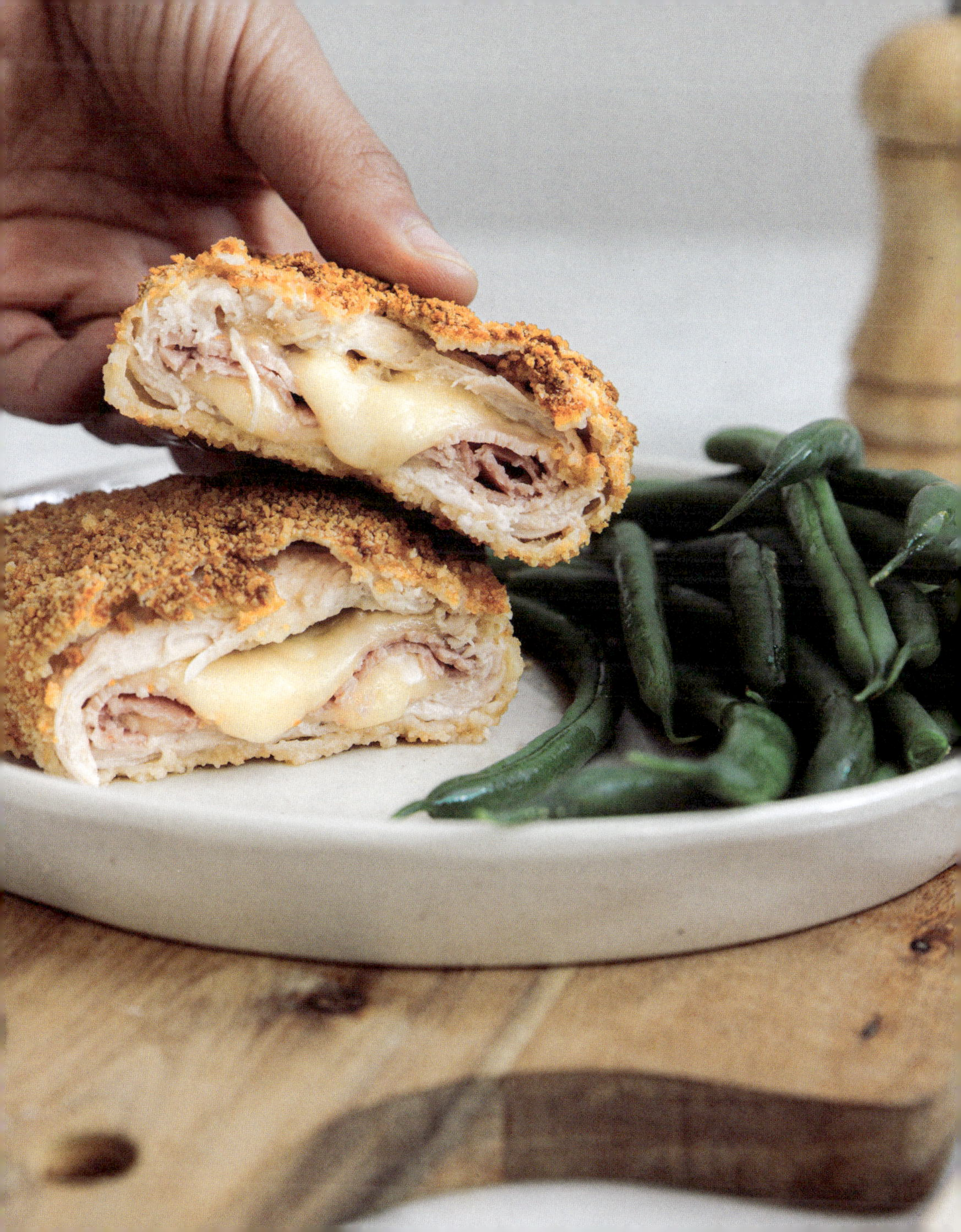

MAKES 12 - MEDIUM - PREPARATION 20 MINUTES - COOKING 7 MINUTES

MINI HAM CROISSANTS

- 2 sheets puff pastry
- 2 tablespoons smooth, creamy ricotta
- Salt and black pepper
- 3 slices ham, chopped
- 60 g (2¼ oz) Swiss or mozzarella cheese, grated
- 1 egg yolk, beaten
- Sesame seeds

1. Cut the puff pastry into 12 triangles. Spread some ricotta on each triangle, then season with salt and pepper.

2. Arrange pieces of ham on top of each triangle, then add the grated Swiss or mozzarella cheese along the long edge.

3. Roll up each triangle from the long edge to the top, bending the points in slightly to form a crescent shape.

4. Place the croissants in the air fryer basket. Brush the tops with beaten egg yolk and sprinkle with a few sesame seeds. Bake for 7 minutes at 190°C (375°F).

TIP
Enjoy these croissants with a nice salad or raw vegetable sticks.

LUNCH & DINNER

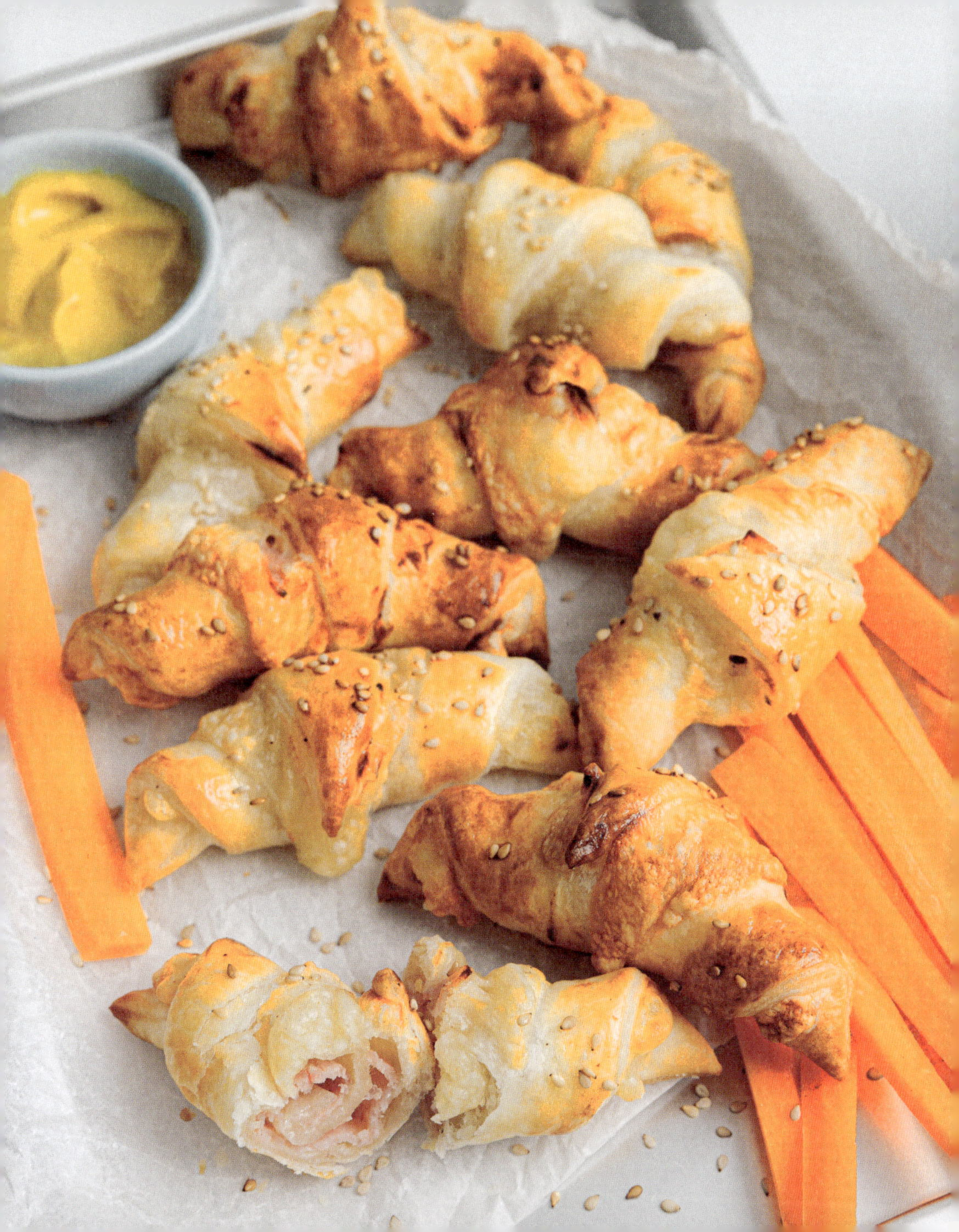

SERVES 2 - MEDIUM - PREPARATION 25 MINUTES - COOKING 30 MINUTES

VEGGIE LASAGNE

- Olive oil
- 6 dried lasagne sheets
- 400 g (14 oz) ratatouille or canned chopped tomatoes
- 100 g (3½ oz) shredded mozzarella cheese

WHITE SAUCE
- 250 ml (9 fl oz) milk
- 20 g (¾ oz) cornflour (cornstarch)
- Grated nutmeg
- Salt and black pepper

1 To make the white sauce, mix the milk and cornflour in a saucepan. Place the saucepan over a medium–high heat and whisk continuously until thickened (about 4 minutes). Season with the nutmeg, salt and pepper, then set aside.

2 Pour a drizzle of olive oil into the base of an air fryer-safe dish or the lined air fryer basket, then place two lasagne sheets side by side on the bottom. Top with ratatouille or tomato, a little white sauce and some shredded mozzarella. Continue with two more layers of lasagne sheets, white sauce, ratatouille or tomato and mozzarella.

3 Cook in the air fryer for 30 minutes at 180°C (350°F).

TIP
You can add beef mince or plant-based mince for a more substantial meal. If adding, brown the mince over a medium heat for 5 minutes first.

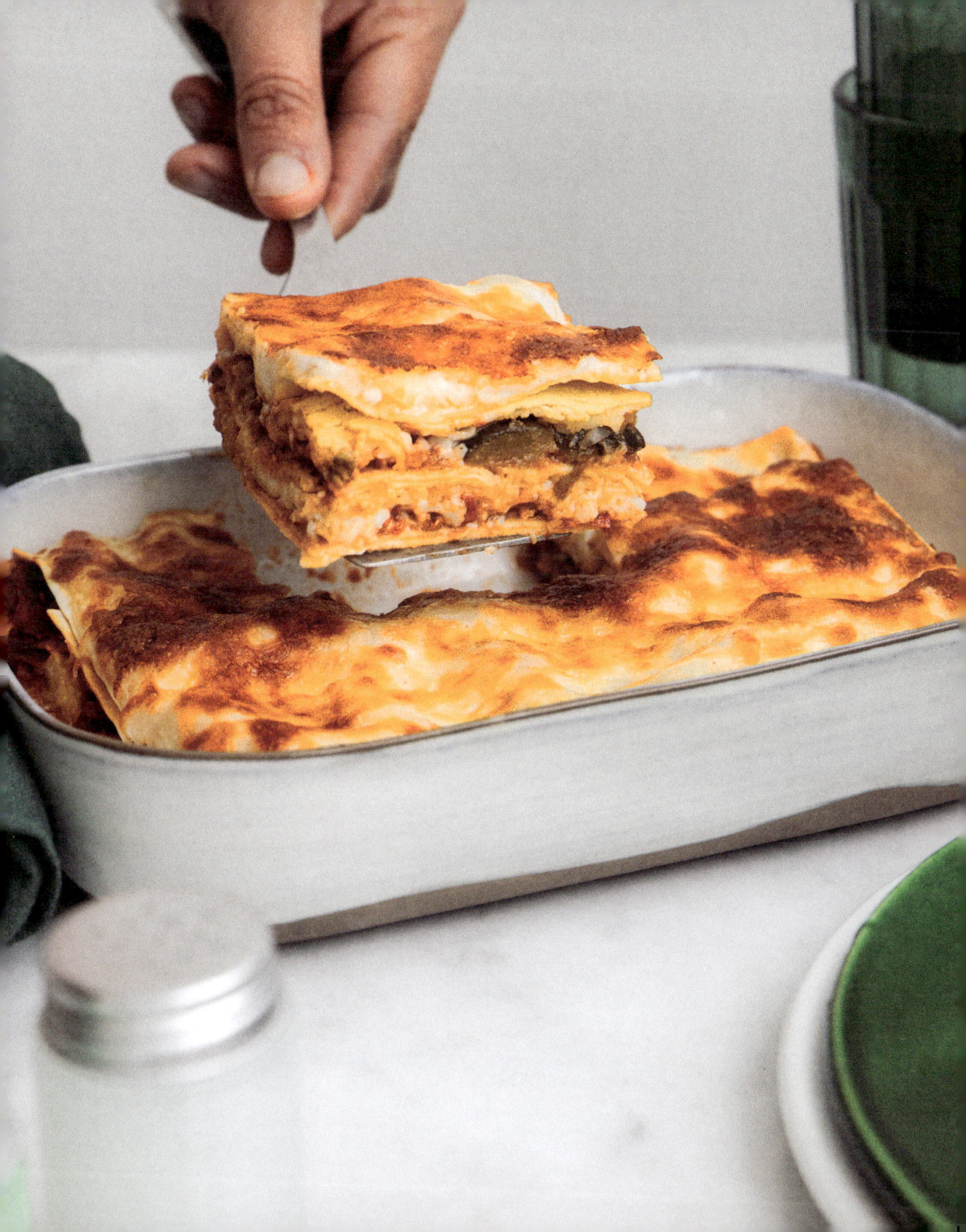

SERVES 2 - EASY - PREPARATION 10 MINUTES - COOKING 10 MINUTES

BRUSCHETTA

- 80 g (2¾ oz) pesto
- 4 slices wholemeal or wholegrain bread
- 2 large tomatoes, sliced
- 1 mozzarella cheese ball, torn into pieces
- 4 slices prosciutto

1 Spread pesto on each slice of bread, then add a couple of tomato slices. Add some mozzarella pieces and top with a little more pesto.

2 Put the bruschetta in the air fryer basket and cook for 10 minutes at 190°C (375°F). Top with prosciutto before serving.

TIP
Serve the bruschetta with a side of rocket (arugula).

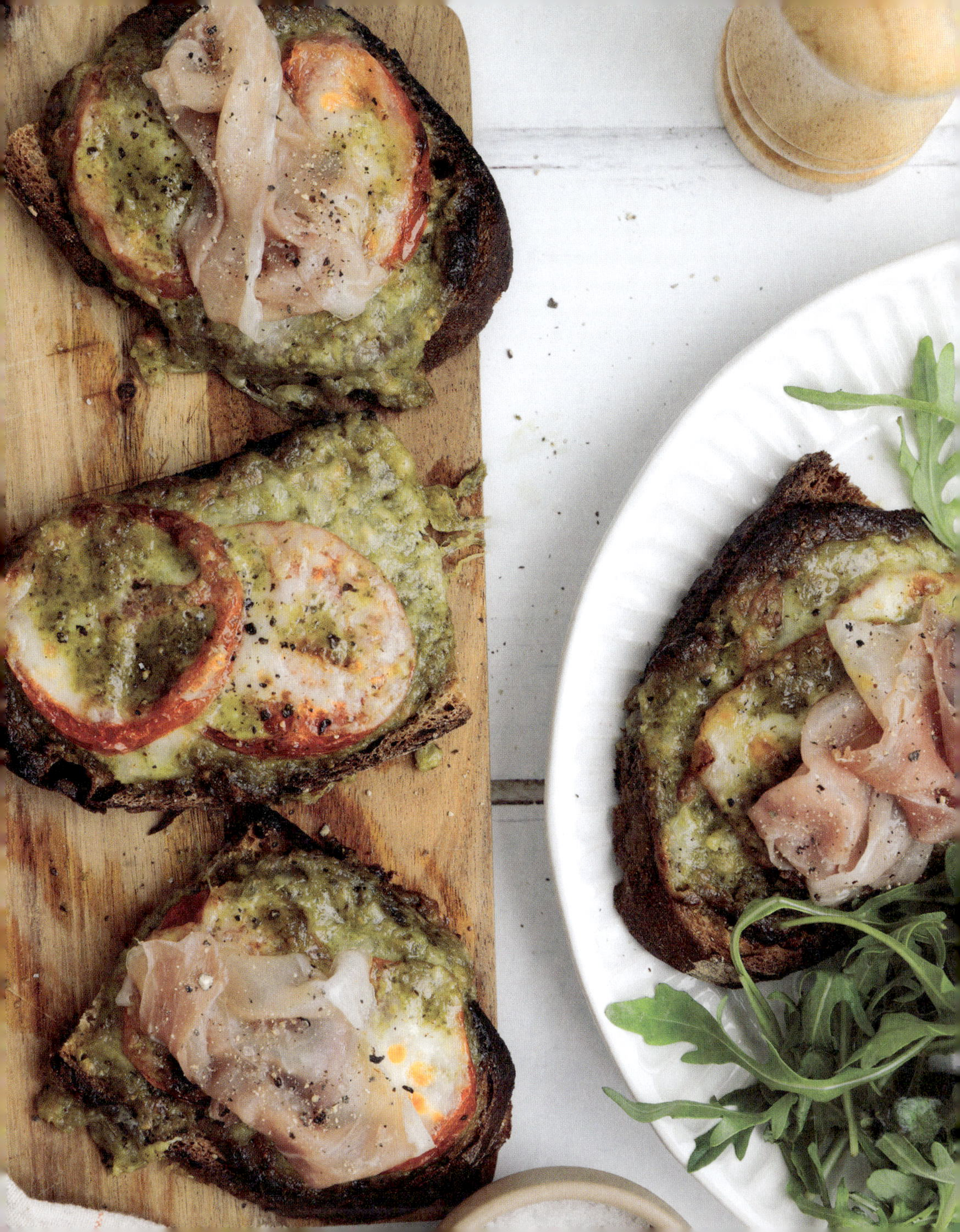

SERVES 2 - ADVANCED - PREPARATION 5 MINUTES - COOKING 2 MINUTES

CRUMBED EGG YOLKS

- 4 eggs
- 80 g (2¾ oz) breadcrumbs
- Salt and black pepper

1 Crack the eggs carefully into a bowl, ensuring not to break any yolks.

2 Place the breadcrumbs in a bowl with some salt and pepper.

3 Using a large spoon, carefully lift the yolks from the bowl, one at a time, and lower them gently into the bowl of breadcrumbs.

4 Gently coat the yolks in the breadcrumbs.

5 Once the yolks are well coated, carefully lower them into the air fryer pan and cook for 2 minutes at 160°C (325°F).

TIP
These crispy crumbed egg yolks with their runny centres are great in salads. Use the leftover whites in the marble cake recipe on page 124.

LUNCH & DINNER

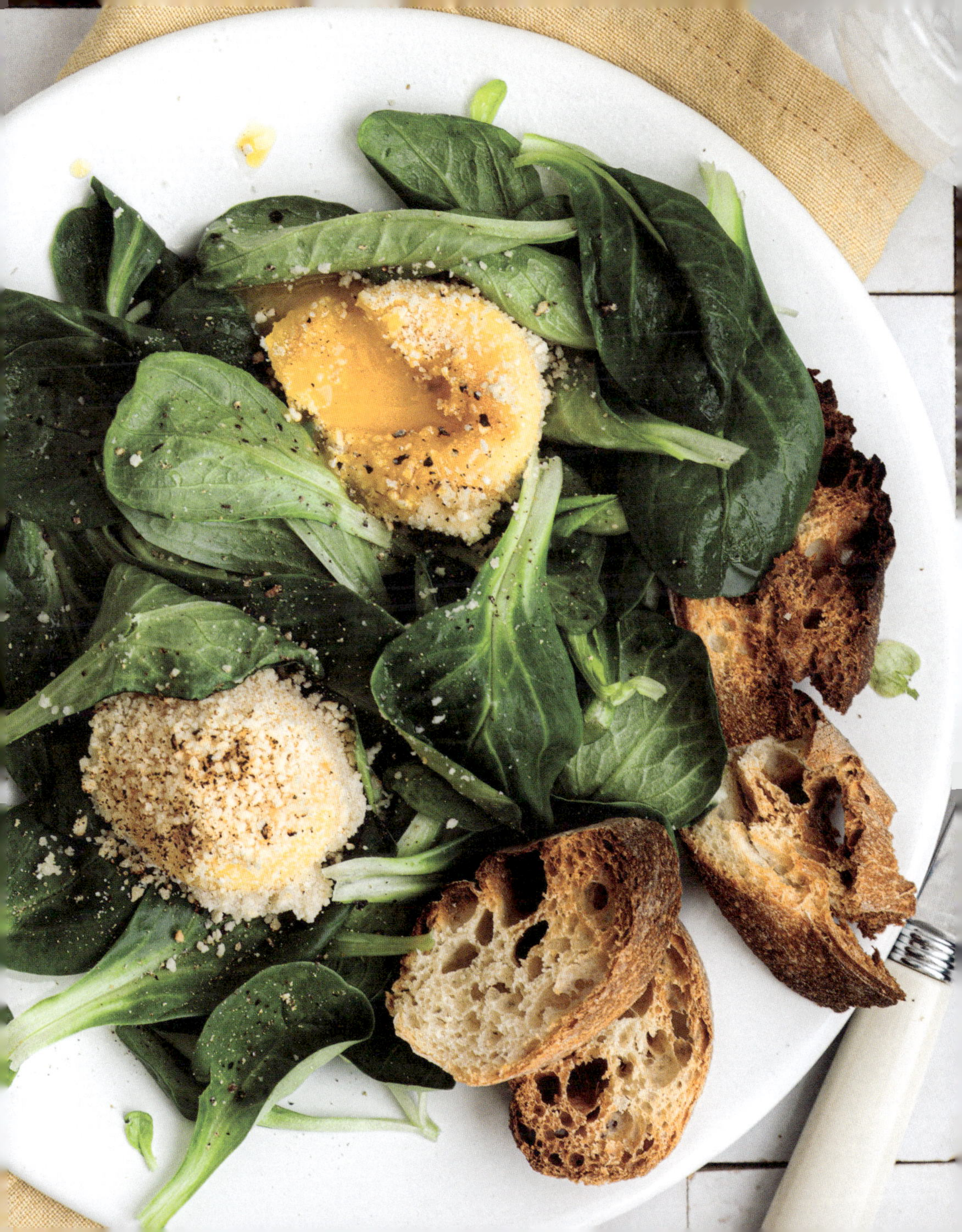

SERVES 2 - MEDIUM - PREPARATION 30 MINUTES - COOKING 30 MINUTES

MEATBALLS & POTATO ROSTI

ROSTI
- 350 g (12 oz) potatoes, peeled
- 1 egg
- ½ onion, peeled and finely chopped
- Big handful of parsley, chopped
- Salt and black pepper
- Spray oil

MEATBALLS
- ½ onion, peeled and finely chopped
- 250 g (9 oz) beef mince
- 1 egg
- 20 g (¾ oz) breadcrumbs
- Big handful of parsley, chopped
- Few sprigs of thyme, leaves only
- Salt and black pepper

- Tomato sauce, to serve

1 To make the rosti, cook the whole potatoes in a saucepan of salted boiling water for 10 minutes. They should still be a little firm. Drain and let cool, then grate the potatoes and place in a bowl. Add the egg, chopped onion and parsley and season with salt and pepper. Stir to combine, then form patties (you can use a biscuit cutter to shape). Spray the air fryer basket with oil, place the patties in the basket and cook for 20 minutes at 180°C (350°F), turning halfway through the cooking time.

2 To make the meatballs, combine all the ingredients in a bowl. Form six balls and place in the air fryer basket. Cook for 10 minutes at 180°C (350°F), turning halfway through the cooking time.

3 Serve the meatballs and rosti with the pasta sauce, heated if desired.

TIP
Serve this dish with a side of rice if you like.

LUNCH & DINNER

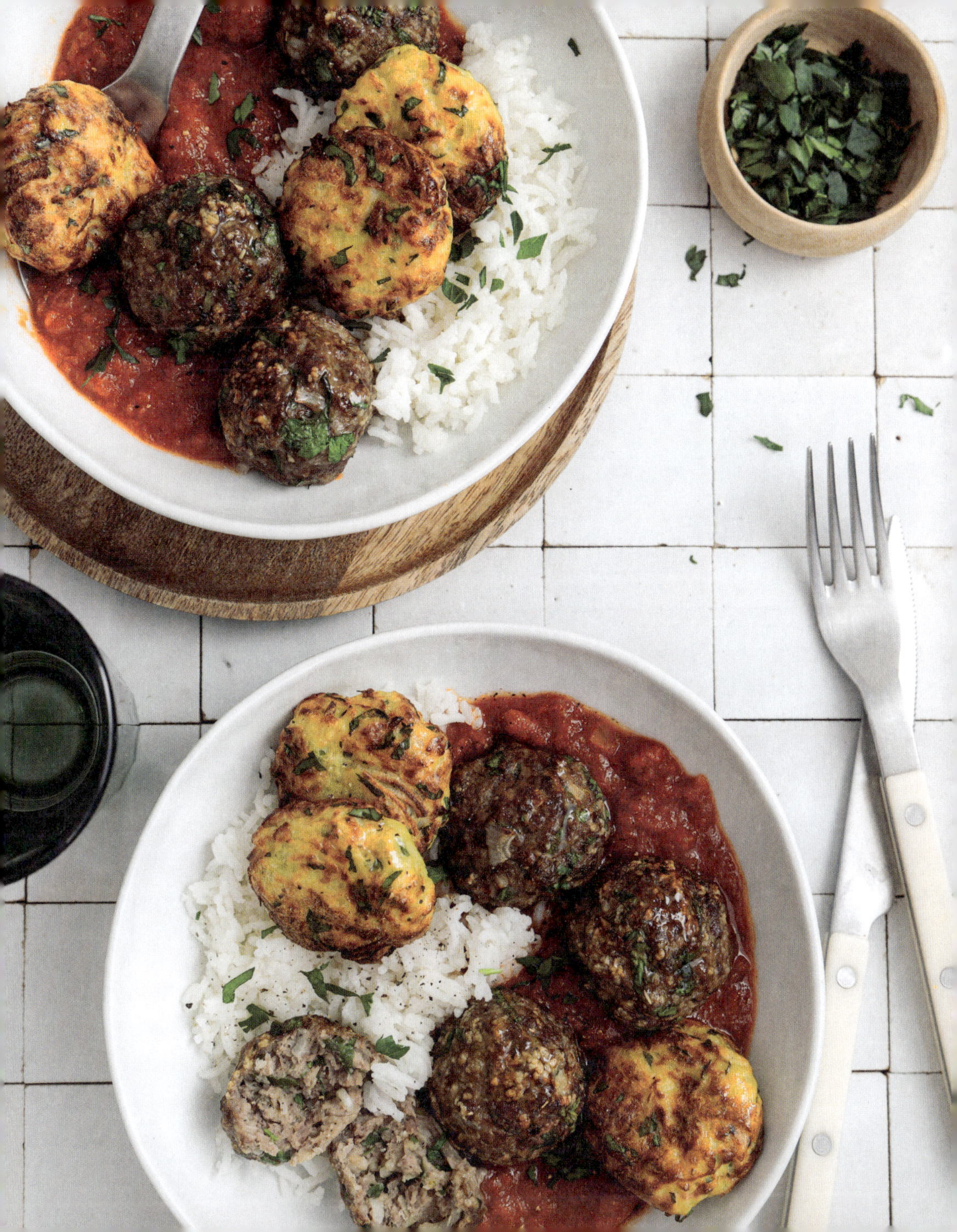

SERVES 2 - EASY - PREPARATION 20 MINUTES - COOKING 25 MINUTES

STUFFED TOMATOES

- 250 g (9 oz) sausage meat
- 20 g (¾ oz) breadcrumbs
- 1 teaspoon ground cumin
- 1 teaspoon paprika
- 1 egg
- Salt and black pepper
- 2 large tomatoes

1 In a bowl, mix the sausage meat together with the breadcrumbs, spices and egg. Season with salt and pepper.

2 Cut the tops off the tomatoes, scoop out the flesh and add it to the filling. Stuff the tomatoes with the filling, put the tops back on and place them in the air fryer basket.

3 Cook for 25 minutes at 180°C (350°F).

TIP
You can also make this recipe with courgettes (zucchini) or mushrooms.

LUNCH & DINNER

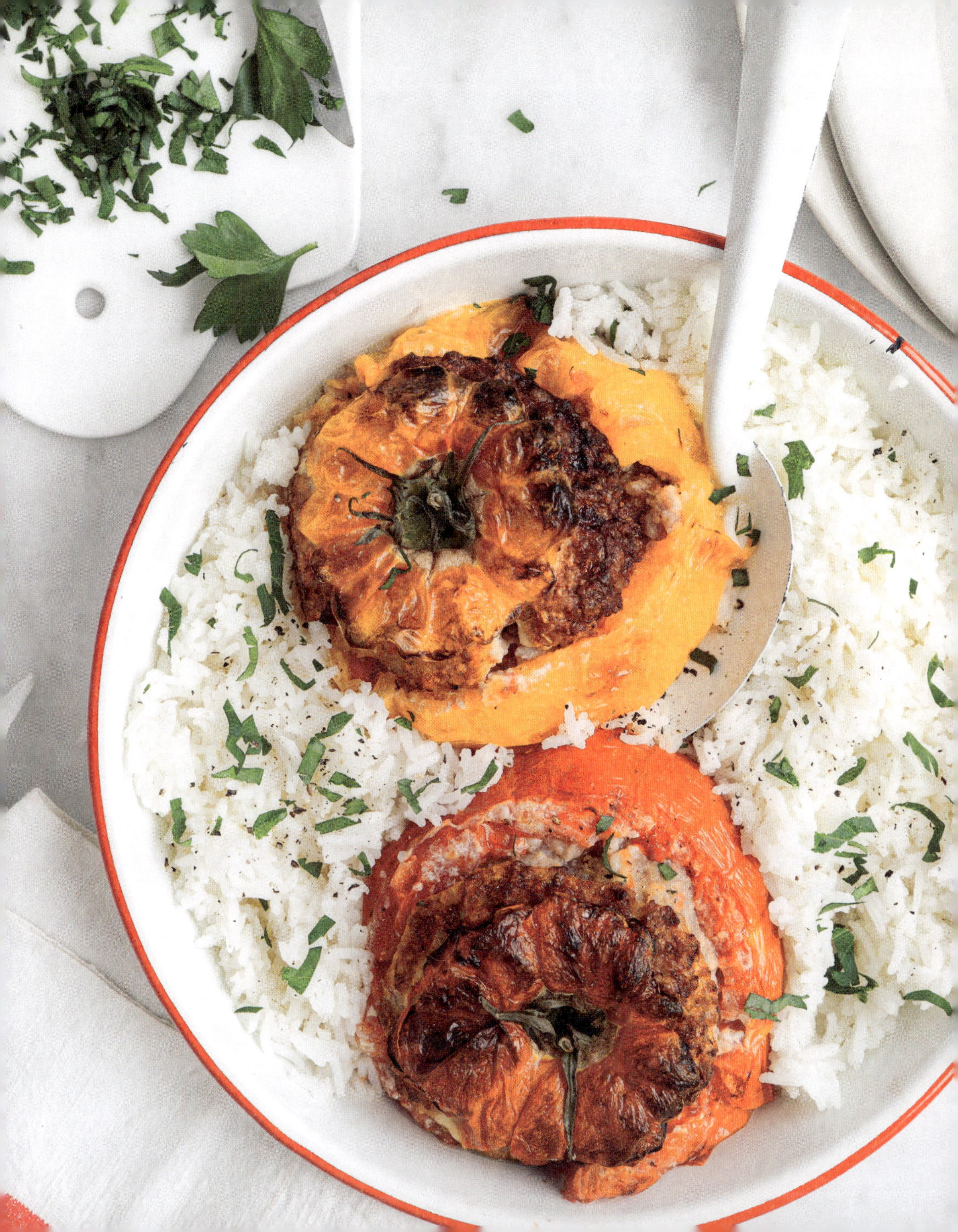

SERVES 2 - EASY - PREPARATION 10 MINUTES - COOKING 20 MINUTES

ROASTED CARROTS

- Handful of baby or Dutch carrots, with tops
- 1 teaspoon soy sauce
- 1 tablespoon honey
- 2 tablespoons olive oil
- 1 tablespoon seeds of your choice, such as sesame

1 Wash the carrots. In a bowl, combine the soy sauce, honey, oil and seeds. Add the carrots and coat well.

2 Place the carrots in the air fryer basket and cook for 20 minutes at 180°C (350°F).

TIP
These carrots pair perfectly with mashed potatoes and a nice grilled steak. It's the perfect side dish for special occasions!

LUNCH & DINNER

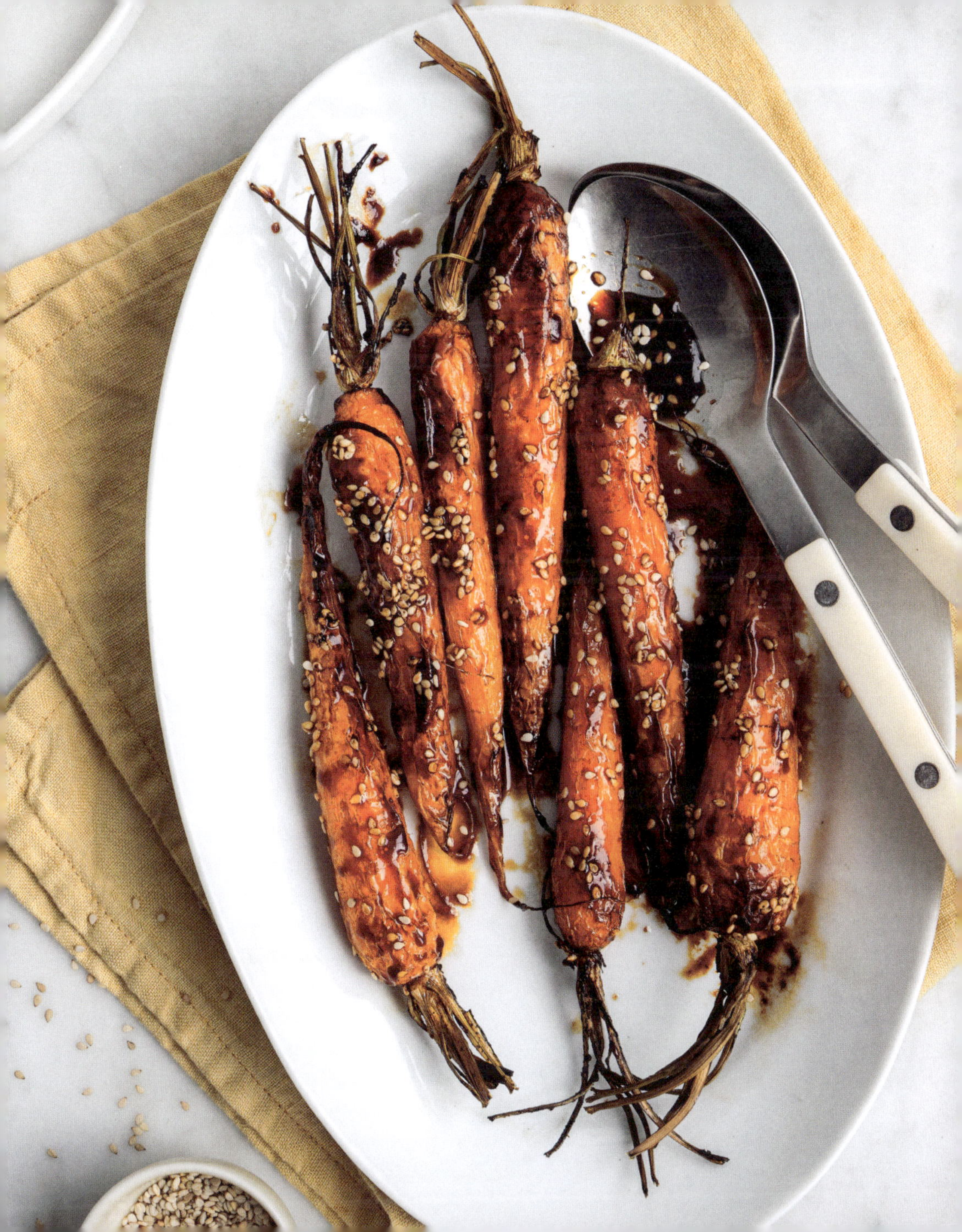

SERVES 2 - MEDIUM - PREPARATION 40 MINUTES - COOKING 12 MINUTES

SPICY CHICKEN SKEWERS

- 2 chicken breasts
- 1 teaspoon garlic powder
- 1 teaspoon paprika
- 1 teaspoon ground turmeric
- 1 teaspoon hot paprika
- 1 tablespoon sunflower or vegetable oil
- 6 metal skewers

SAUCE
- 100 g (3½ oz) cream cheese or sour cream
- 1 tablespoon chopped chives
- 2 tablespoons chopped parsley
- 1 tablespoon lemon juice
- Salt and black pepper

1 Cut the chicken into 2-3 cm (¾-1¼ inch) cubes and put them in a bowl. Add all the spices and the oil. Mix well and allow to marinate for 30 minutes in the refrigerator.

2 Meanwhile, make the sauce by combining all the sauce ingredients in a bowl. Set aside in the refrigerator.

3 Thread the marinated chicken cubes onto the skewers. Place them in the air fryer basket and cook for 12 minutes at 180°C (350°F), turning halfway through the cooking time. Serve with the sauce.

TIP
Serve the skewers with some rocket (arugula) on the side.

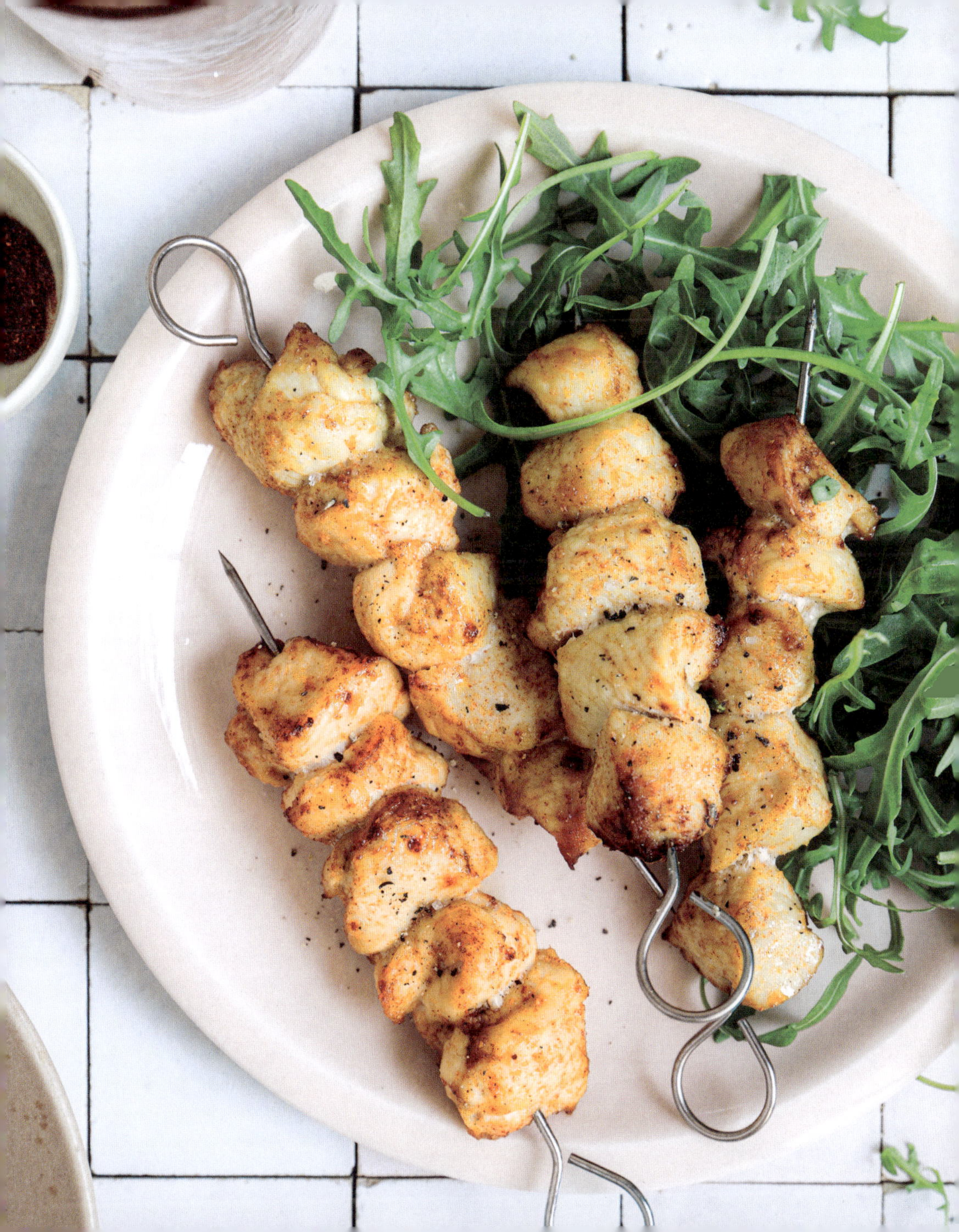

MAKES 8 - MEDIUM - PREPARATION 20 MINUTES - COOKING 10 MINUTES

BEEF SAMOSAS

- 150 g (5½ oz) beef mince
- ½ onion, peeled and finely chopped
- Spray oil
- 1 tablespoon tomato paste (concentrated purée)
- 1 teaspoon chilli powder
- 1 teaspoon paprika
- 1 teaspoon garlic powder
- 1 teaspoon ground cumin
- Salt and black pepper
- 4 sheets brik or filo (phyllo) pastry
- Melted butter (optional)
- Sunflower or vegetable oil or 1 egg, for brushing

1 Brown the beef mince and onion in a lightly oiled frying pan over a medium heat. Once cooked, add the tomato paste as well as the spices, salt and pepper.

2 Cut the pastry sheets in half. If using brik pastry, fold the rounded edge over to the other edge to make a rectangle. If using filo pastry, brush with melted butter. Place a dollop of meat filling at the bottom of each half. Fold the pastry over diagonally to form a triangle, then continue folding the parcel in a triangle shape to the end.

3 Brush the parcels with a little melted butter, oil or beaten egg using a pastry brush and air fry for 10 minutes at 180°C (350°F).

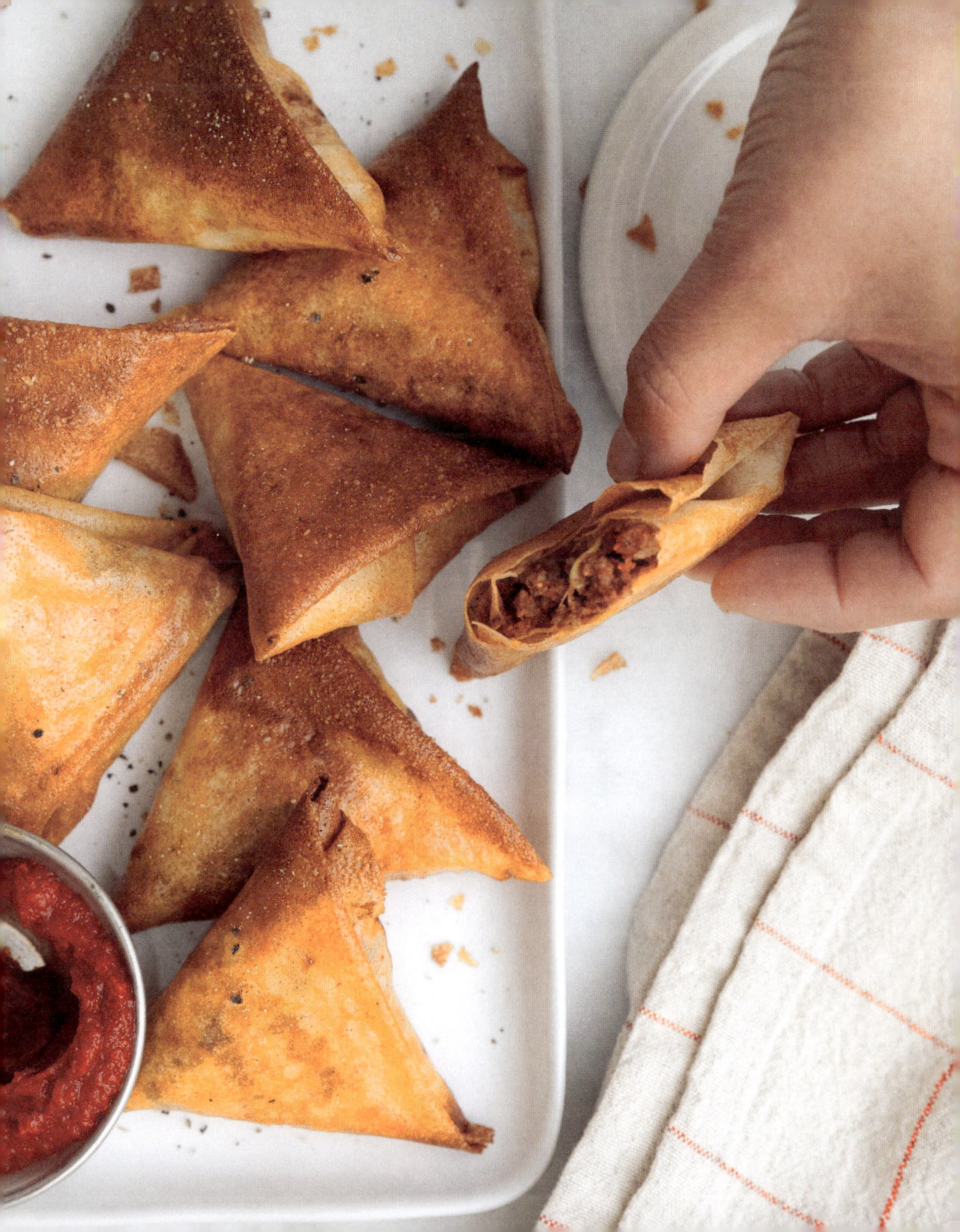

SERVES 2 - MEDIUM - PREPARATION 20 MINUTES - COOKING 10 MINUTES

BAKED COD

- ½ yellow pepper (capsicum), seeds and core removed, finely diced
- 1 tomato, finely diced
- 1 courgette (zucchini), finely diced
- Big handful of chopped parsley
- Salt and black pepper
- Lemon juice
- Olive oil
- 2 cod fillets

1 In a bowl, combine the diced vegetables, parsley, salt, pepper, a squeeze of lemon juice and a drizzle of olive oil and mix well.

2 Spread the vegetables out on a sheet of baking paper and place the cod fillets on top. Season the fish with salt and pepper, a drizzle of olive oil and a squeeze of lemon juice. Fold the baking paper over to form a parcel and secure by twisting the ends tightly to seal.

3 Place the parcel in the air fryer pan and cook for 10 minutes at 180°C (350°F).

TIP
Serve with rice for a nutritious and balanced meal.

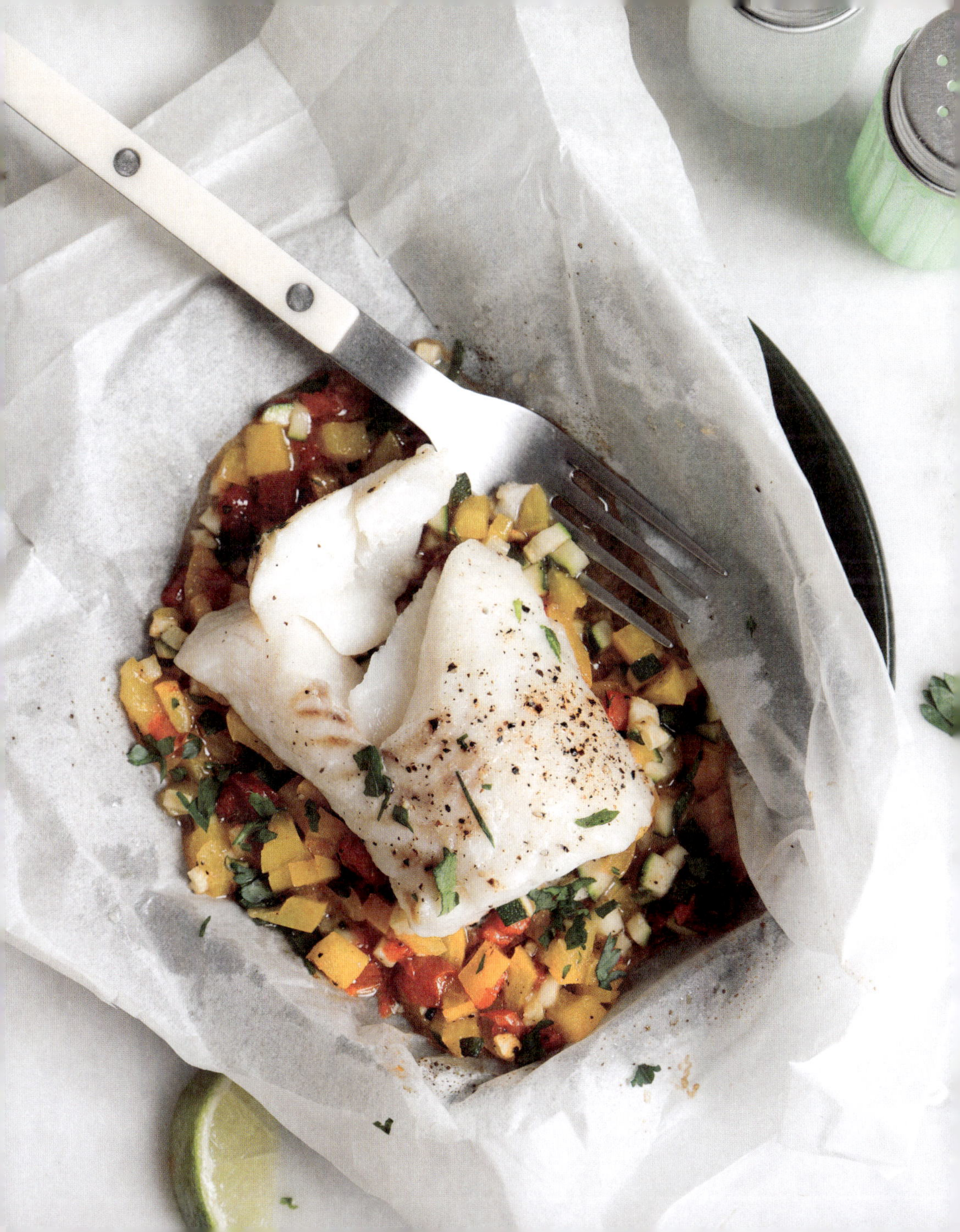

SERVES 2 - EASY - PREPARATION 10 MINUTES - COOKING 20 MINUTES

ROASTED VEGETABLE FRIES

- 400 g (14 oz) vegetables of your choice, such as parsnips, butternut squash, pumpkin and carrot
- 1 tablespoon olive oil
- Spices of your choice, such as ground turmeric, ground cumin, garlic powder and paprika, to taste
- Salt and black pepper

1 Peel the vegetables and cut into fries. Place the fries in a bowl and toss with the olive oil and spices. Season with salt and pepper.

2 Place the fries in the air fryer basket and select the 'fry' mode if available, otherwise cook for 20 minutes at 180°C (350°F).

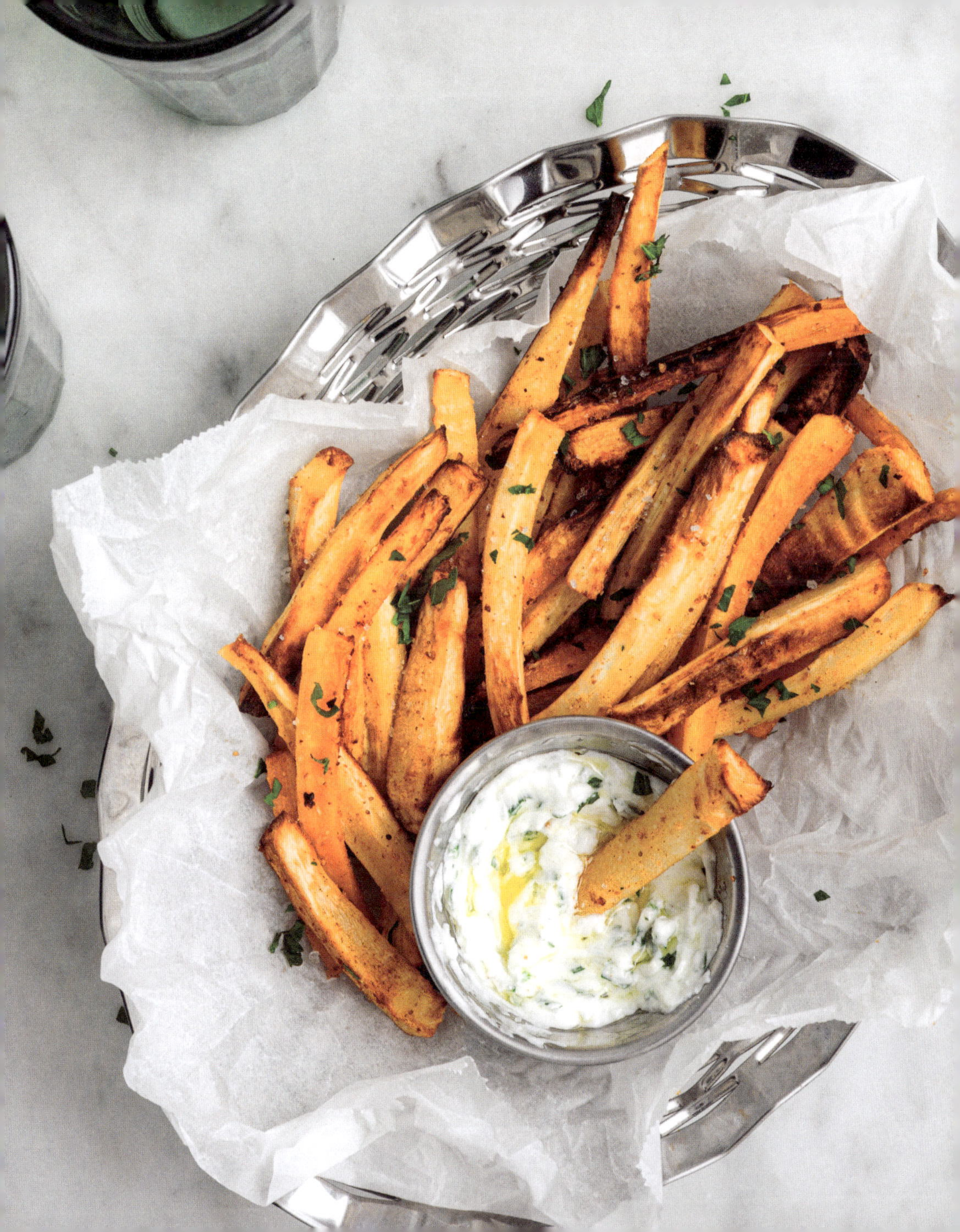

SERVES 2 - EASY - PREPARATION 15 MINUTES - COOKING 10 MINUTES

FRITTATA WITH RED PEPPER

- 4 eggs
- ½ red pepper (capsicum), seeds and core removed, cut into strips
- 2 handfuls of baby spinach leaves
- Salt and black pepper
- 60 g (2¼ oz) shredded mozzarella cheese
- 40 g (1½ oz) Cheddar cheese, grated

1. Line the air fryer basket with baking paper or use an air fryer-safe mould.

2. Break the eggs into a bowl, whisk them and pour them into the lined air fryer basket or mould.

3. Add the chopped pepper and baby spinach leaves. Season with salt and pepper. Sprinkle with the mozzarella and Cheddar cheese and cook for 10 minutes at 180°C (350°F).

TIP
Serve the frittata with lightly toasted bread.

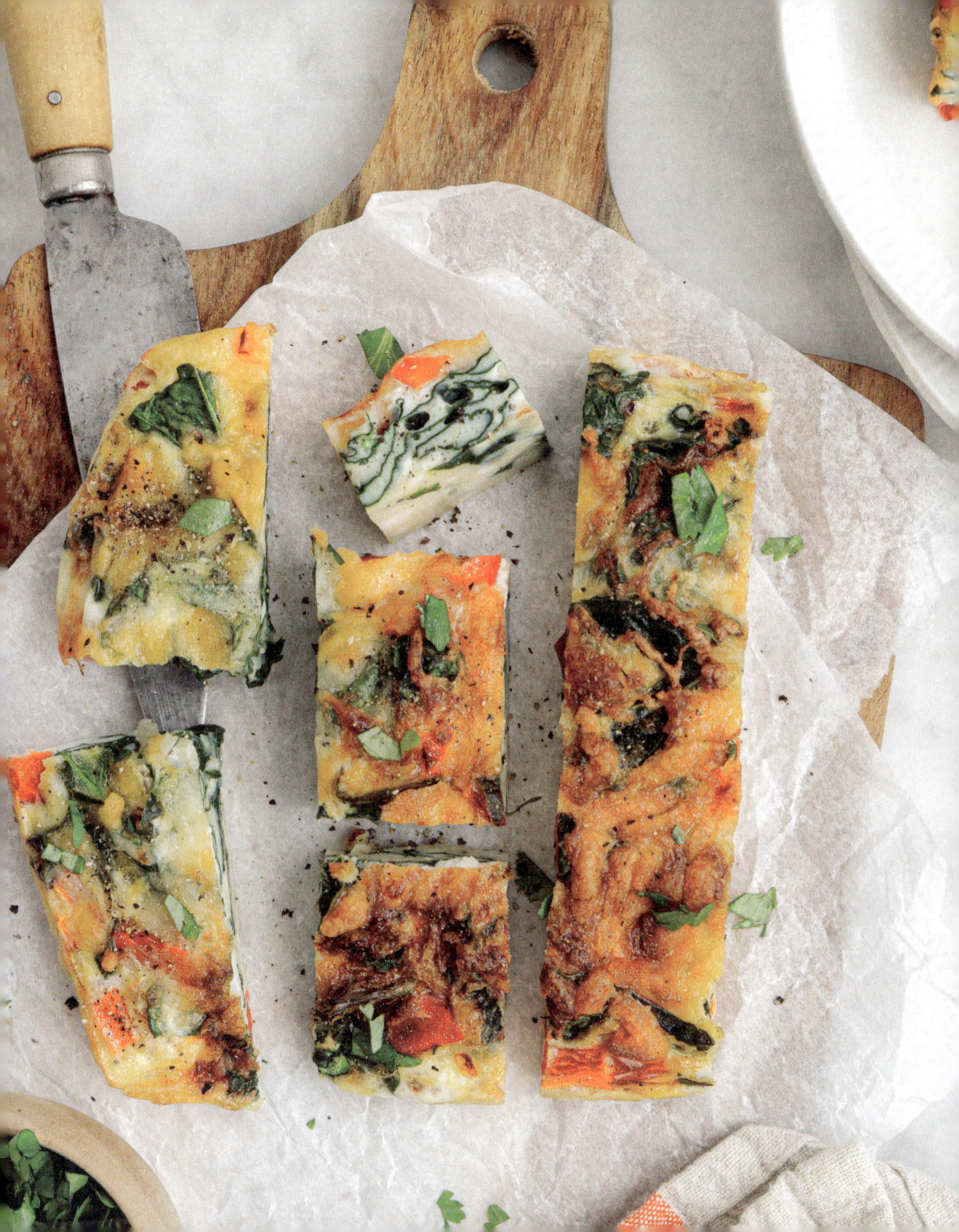

SERVES 2 - EASY - PREPARATION 15 MINUTES - COOKING 20 MINUTES

ROASTED SUMMER VEGETABLES

- 2 red peppers (capsicums), seeds and cores removed
- 1 courgette (zucchini)
- 1 aubergine (eggplant)
- Olive oil
- 1 stalk of thyme
- 1 bay leaf
- 1 sprig of rosemary
- 1 garlic clove, unpeeled
- Salt and black pepper

1 Cut the vegetables into matchsticks, slices, cubes or any other shape you like. In a mixing bowl, toss the vegetables with a drizzle of olive oil, the herbs, garlic and some salt and pepper.

2 Bake for 20 minutes at 200°C (400°F) directly in the air fryer basket or in an air fryer-safe dish.

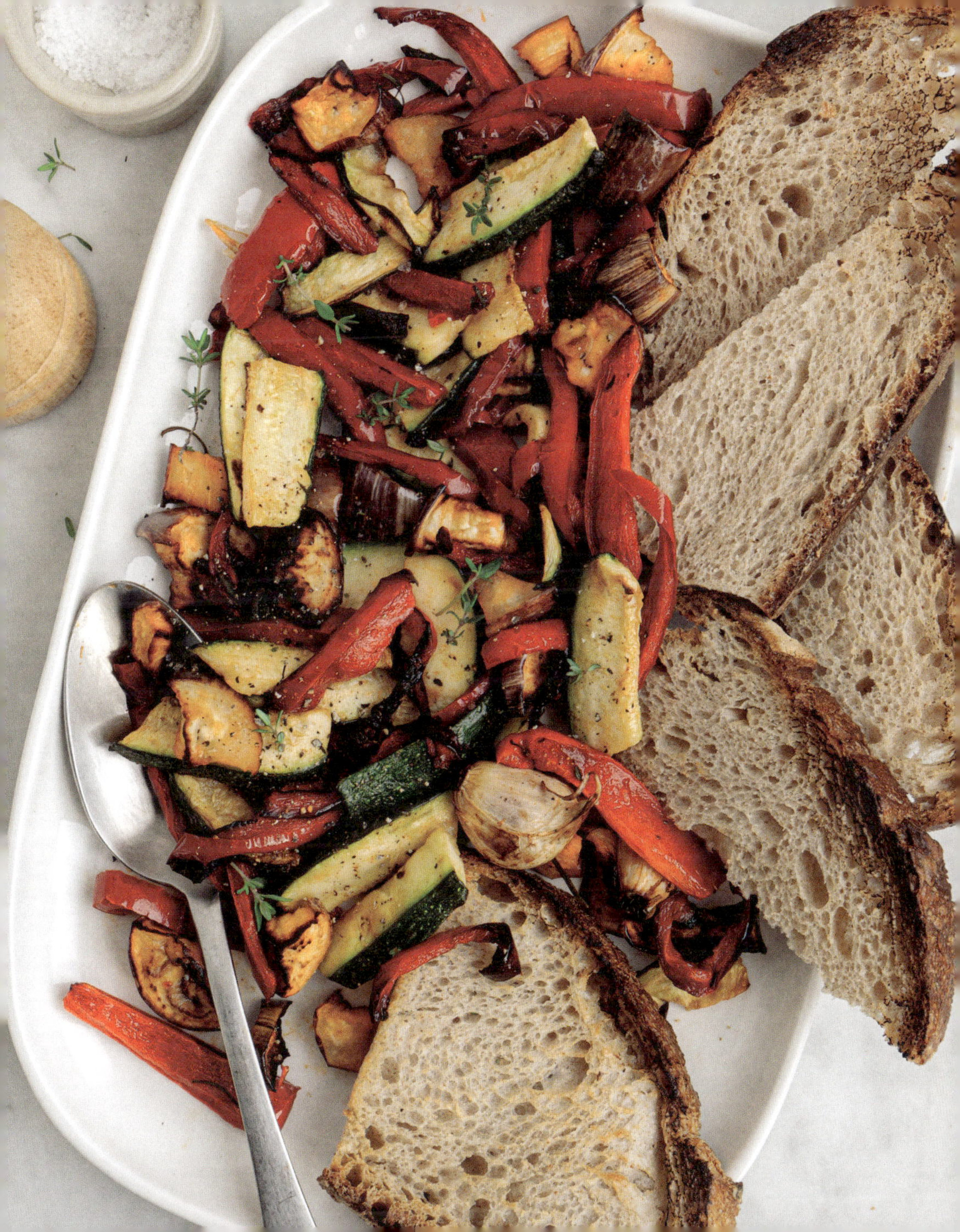

DESSERT

Chocolate muffins	**114**	Banana muffins	**126**
Chocolate cake	**116**	Oat cookies	**128**
Chocolate chip cookies	**118**	Fondant cookies	**130**
Apple crumble muffins	**120**	Almond cake	**132**
Baked apples	**122**	Peanut banana cookies	**134**
Marble cake	**124**	Mug cake	**136**

MAKES 4 - EASY - PREPARATION 15 MINUTES - COOKING 18 MINUTES

CHOCOLATE MUFFINS

- 60 g (2¼ oz) dark chocolate
- 60 g (2¼ oz) butter
- 60 g (2¼ oz) granulated (white) sugar
- 1 egg
- 40 g (1½ oz) plain (all-purpose) flour
- 1 teaspoon baking powder

1 Melt the chocolate with the butter for 2 minutes in an air fryer-safe bowl in the air fryer or microwave, stirring every 30 seconds.

2 Pour the chocolate butter mixture into a bowl and add the sugar, egg, flour and baking powder. Stir well to form a smooth batter.

3 Pour the mixture into four silicone or paper muffin cases or ramekins and bake in the air fryer for 18 minutes at 180°C (350°F).

TIP
Add a square of chocolate to the centre of each muffin for a fondant version.

DESSERT

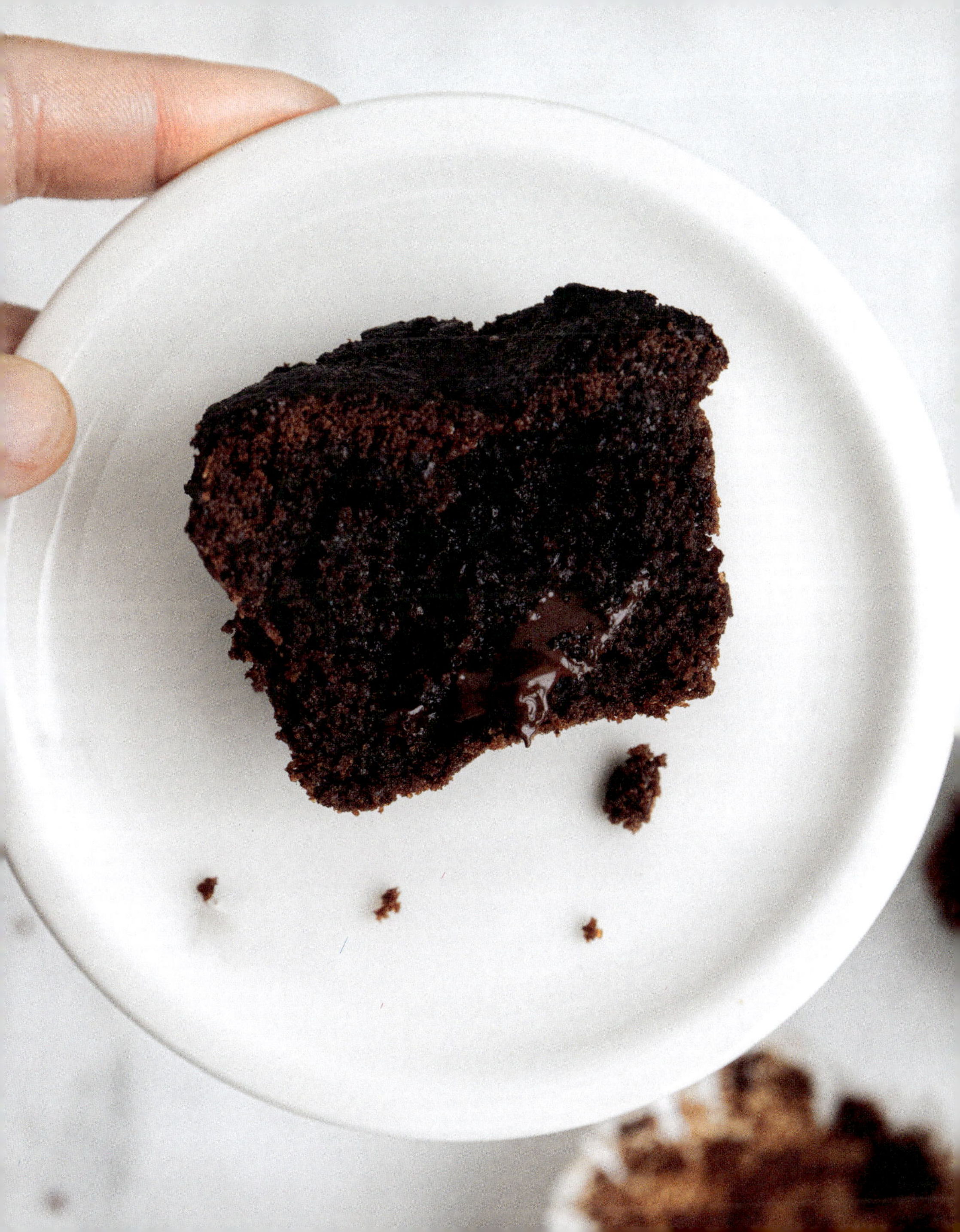

SERVES 4 - EASY - PREPARATION 15 MINUTES - COOKING 30 MINUTES

CHOCOLATE CAKE

- 60 g (2¼ oz) butter
- 100 g (3½ oz) dark cooking chocolate
- 50 g (1¾ oz) granulated (white) sugar
- 2 teaspoons vanilla sugar or 1 teaspoon vanilla extract
- 50 g (1¾ oz) plain (all-purpose) flour
- 2 eggs
- Sea salt, to taste (optional)

1 Melt the butter and chocolate in an air fryer-safe bowl in the air fryer at 100°C (200°F) for 2 minutes.

2 Meanwhile, combine the sugar, vanilla sugar or extract and flour in a bowl. Add the eggs, then the melted chocolate and butter and mix.

3 Pour the batter into an air fryer-safe dish that is approximately 20 cm (8 inches) in diameter and cook for 25 minutes at 160°C (325°F).

4 Allow to cool, then remove the cake from the dish and sprinkle with a little sea salt to serve.

TIP
You can replace the butter with apple purée for a lighter version (but do not melt the chocolate with the purée).

DESSERT

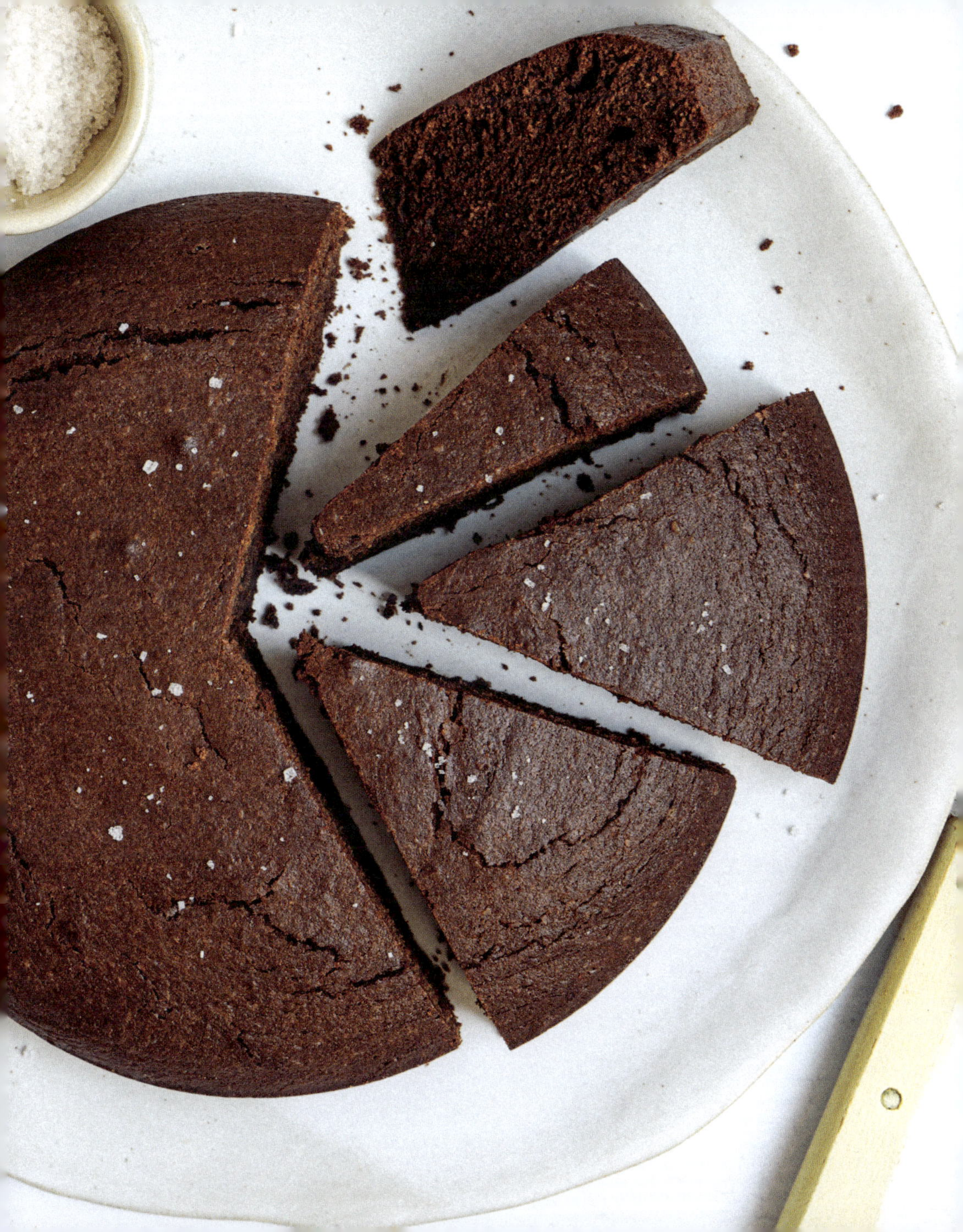

MAKES ABOUT 15 - EASY - PREPARATION 15 MINUTES - COOKING 10 MINUTES

CHOCOLATE CHIP COOKIES

- 125 g (4½ oz) softened butter
- 1 egg
- 125 g (4½ oz) raw or light brown sugar
- 200 g (7 oz) plain (all-purpose) flour
- 100 g (3½ oz) chocolate chips
- ½ teaspoon baking powder
- Pinch of salt
- 1 teaspoon vanilla extract

1 In a bowl, beat the butter using an electric beater until creamy. Beat in the egg and then use a spatula or wooden spoon to mix in the remaining ingredients.

2 Form a log with the dough, then cut it into 15 slices, each 1 cm (½ inch) thick.

3 Place the cookies in the air fryer pan and bake for 10 minutes at 200°C (400°F).

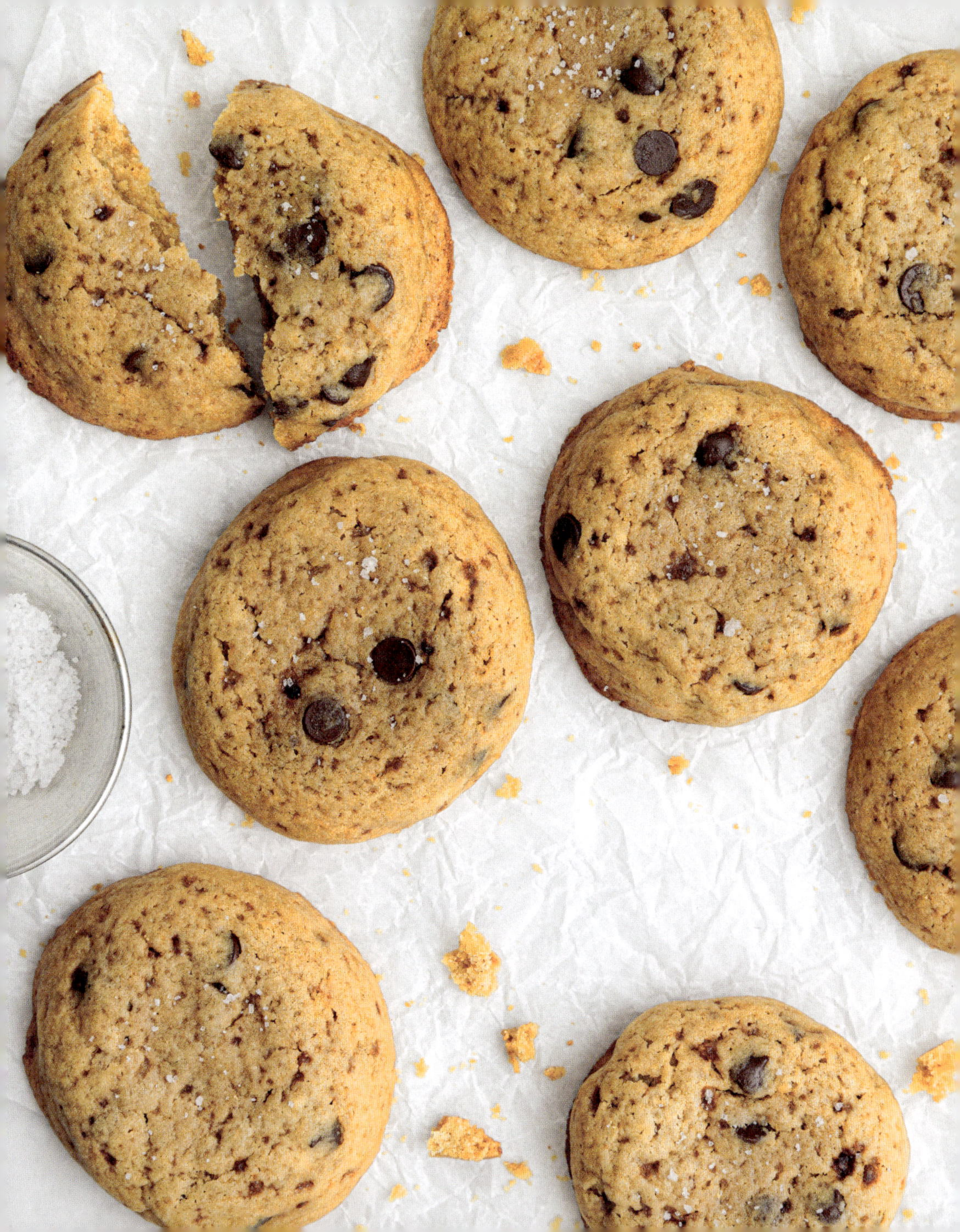

MAKES 4 - MEDIUM - PREPARATION 20 MINUTES - COOKING 20 MINUTES

APPLE CRUMBLE MUFFINS

MUFFINS
- 1 egg
- 150 g (5½ oz) skyr or Greek yoghurt
- 60 g (2¼ oz) plain (all-purpose) flour
- 10 g (¼ oz) softened butter or sunflower or vegetable oil
- 1 teaspoon baking powder
- 1 apple, peeled, cored and finely diced

CRUMBLE
- 10 g (¼ oz) softened butter
- 25 g (1 oz) plain (all-purpose) flour
- 20 g (¾ oz) chocolate, chopped

1. In a bowl, mix the egg with the skyr or yoghurt, flour, butter or oil and baking powder. Add the diced apple. Mix well and set aside.

2. Make the crumble by mixing the softened butter with the flour and chocolate.

3. Pour the muffin mixture into four silicone or paper muffin cases or ramekins and sprinkle with the chocolate crumble topping. Cook in the air fryer for 20 minutes at 180°C (350°F).

TIP
The crumble topping is optional — you can make this recipe without it.

DESSERT

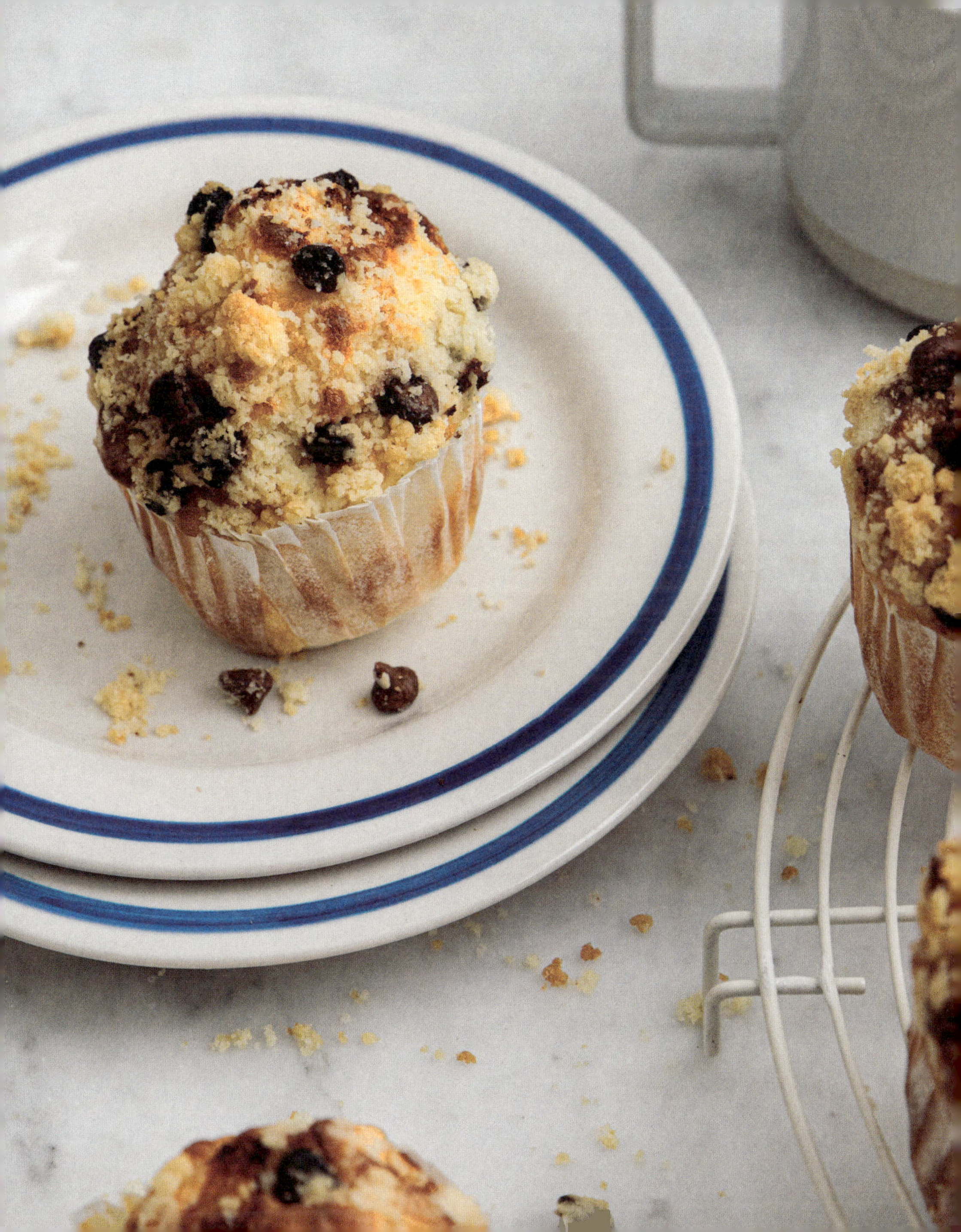

SERVES 2 - EASY - PREPARATION 10 MINUTES - COOKING 10 MINUTES

BAKED APPLES

- 2 large apples, peeled, cored and thinly sliced
- 1 tablespoon water
- 1 tablespoon granulated (white) sugar

1 Line the air fryer basket with baking paper, then place the stacks of sliced apples in the basket.

2 Pour 1 tablespoon of water over the apples into the bottom of the basket and sprinkle with the sugar. Cook for 10 minutes at 180°C (350°F).

TIP
For a more gourmet version, omit the sugar and pour salted caramel sauce over the apples once cooked.

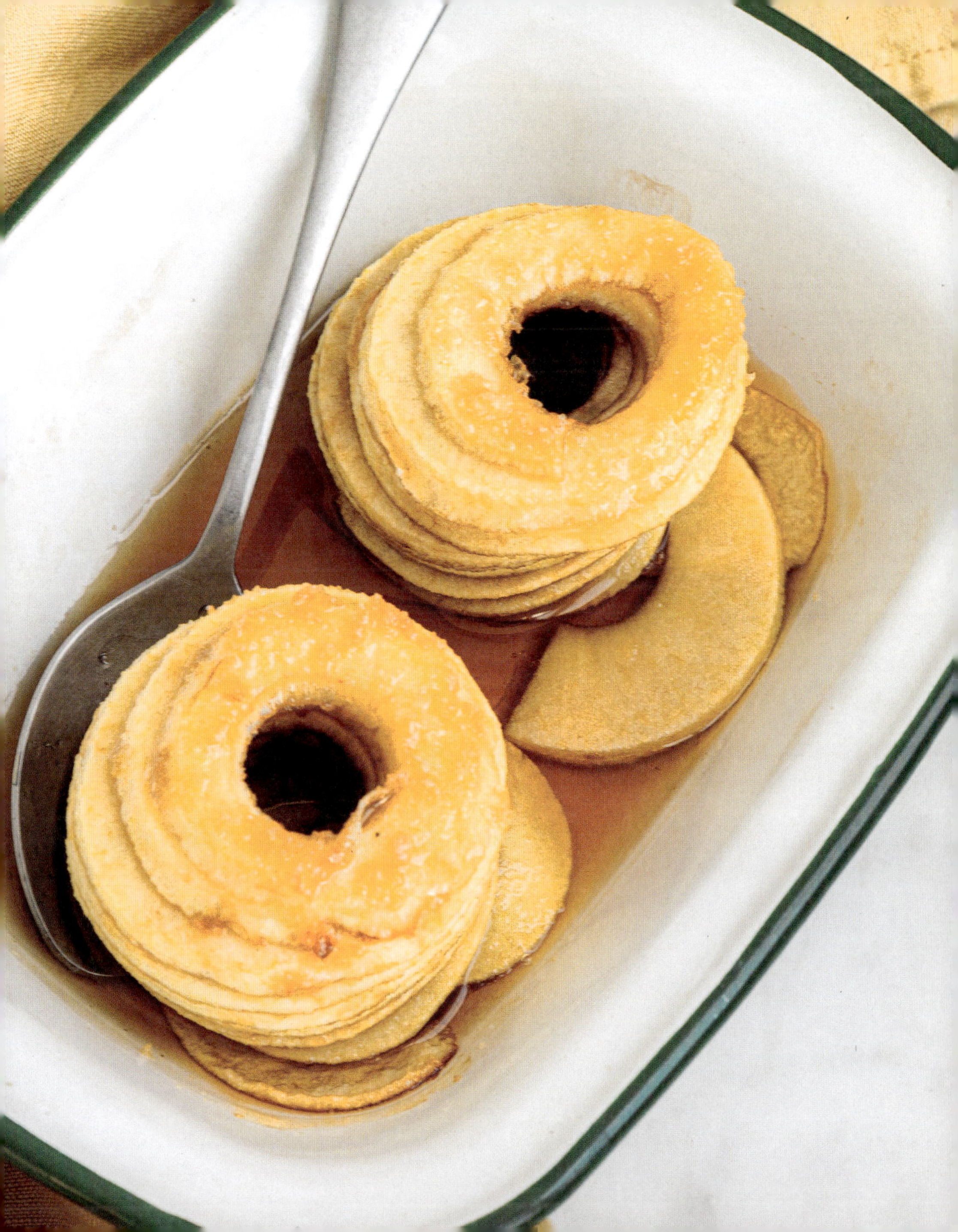

SERVES 6 - ADVANCED - PREPARATION 25 MINUTES - COOKING 20–40 MINUTES

MARBLE CAKE

- 3 egg whites
- 120 g (4¼ oz) ground or fine-cut oat bran
- 125 g (4½ oz) skyr or Greek yoghurt
- 40 g (1½ oz) granulated (white) sugar
- 2 teaspoons baking powder
- 1 teaspoon vanilla extract
- 20 g (¾ oz) chocolate
- 20 g (¾ oz) cocoa powder
- Spray oil

1 Whisk the egg whites using an electric beater until stiff peaks form. Then add the oat bran, skyr or yoghurt, sugar, baking powder and vanilla extract. Separate this batter into two mixing bowls.

2 Melt the chocolate in the microwave in 20- to 30-second bursts. Stir the melted chocolate and cocoa through one portion of the batter.

3 Spread a layer of plain batter into a greased air fryer-safe pan (either one larger pan or multiple smaller pans), then alternate with layers of chocolate and plain batter. Bake at 180°C (350°F) for 20 minutes if using smaller pans, or 30 to 40 minutes if using one large pan.

DESSERT

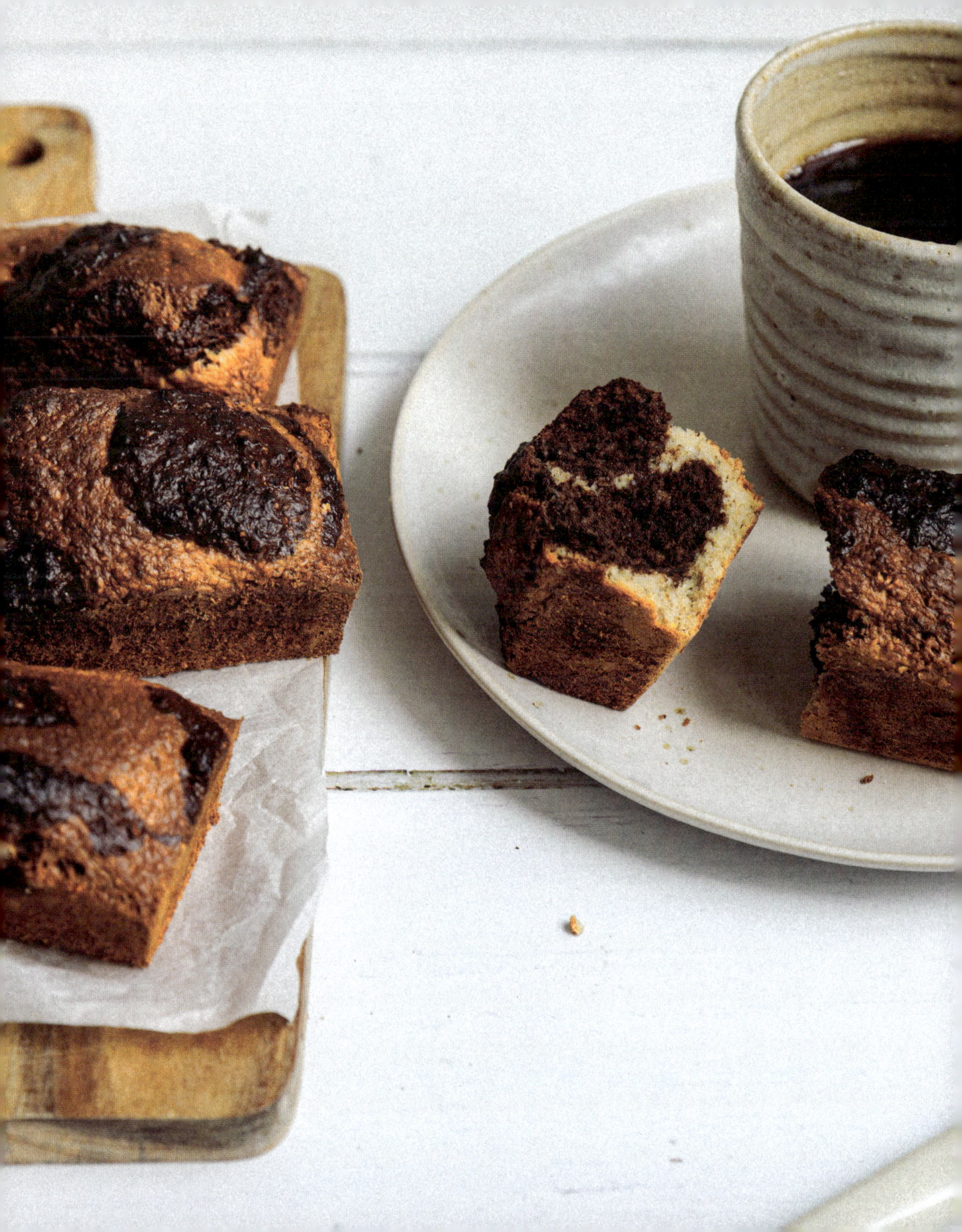

MAKES 4 - EASY - PREPARATION 15 MINUTES - COOKING 20 MINUTES

BANANA MUFFINS

- 1 banana, peeled and chopped
- 1 tablespoon milk
- 50 g (1¾ oz) skyr or Greek yoghurt
- 20 g (¾ oz) nut butter of your choice
- 70 g (2½ oz) plain (all-purpose) flour
- 1 teaspoon baking powder
- 20 g (¾ oz) chocolate, chopped

1 In a bowl, combine the banana, milk, skyr or yoghurt and nut butter.

2 Add the flour and baking powder and stir, then mix in the chopped chocolate pieces.

3 Pour the batter into four silicone or paper muffin cases or ramekins and cook in the air fryer for 20 minutes at 170°C (350°F).

TIP
If you don't like bananas, you can replace them with 100 g (3½ oz) apple purée.

DESSERT

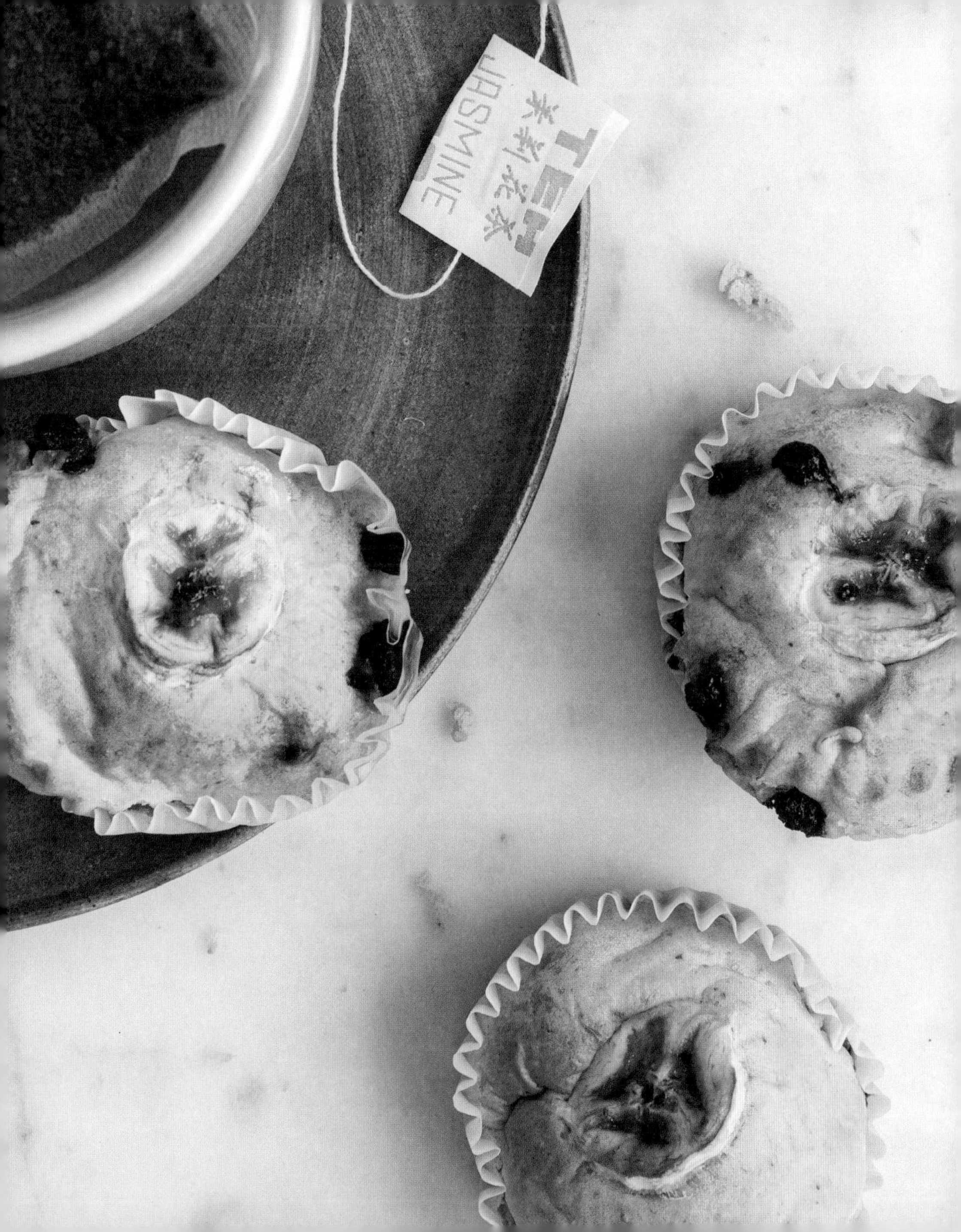
TEA
茉莉花茶
JASMINE

MAKES ABOUT 20 - EASY - PREPARATION 15 MINUTES - COOKING 12 MINUTES

OAT COOKIES

- 100 g (3½ oz) rolled or porridge oats
- 1 egg
- 100 g (3½ oz) apple purée
- 10 g (¼ oz) vanilla sugar
- 20 g (¾ oz) butter or sunflower or vegetable oil
- 20 g (¾ oz) chocolate chips

1 In a bowl, mix all the ingredients to form a dough, then make small balls and flatten them down a little.

2 Place the cookies in the air fryer basket and bake for 12 minutes at 180°C (350°F).

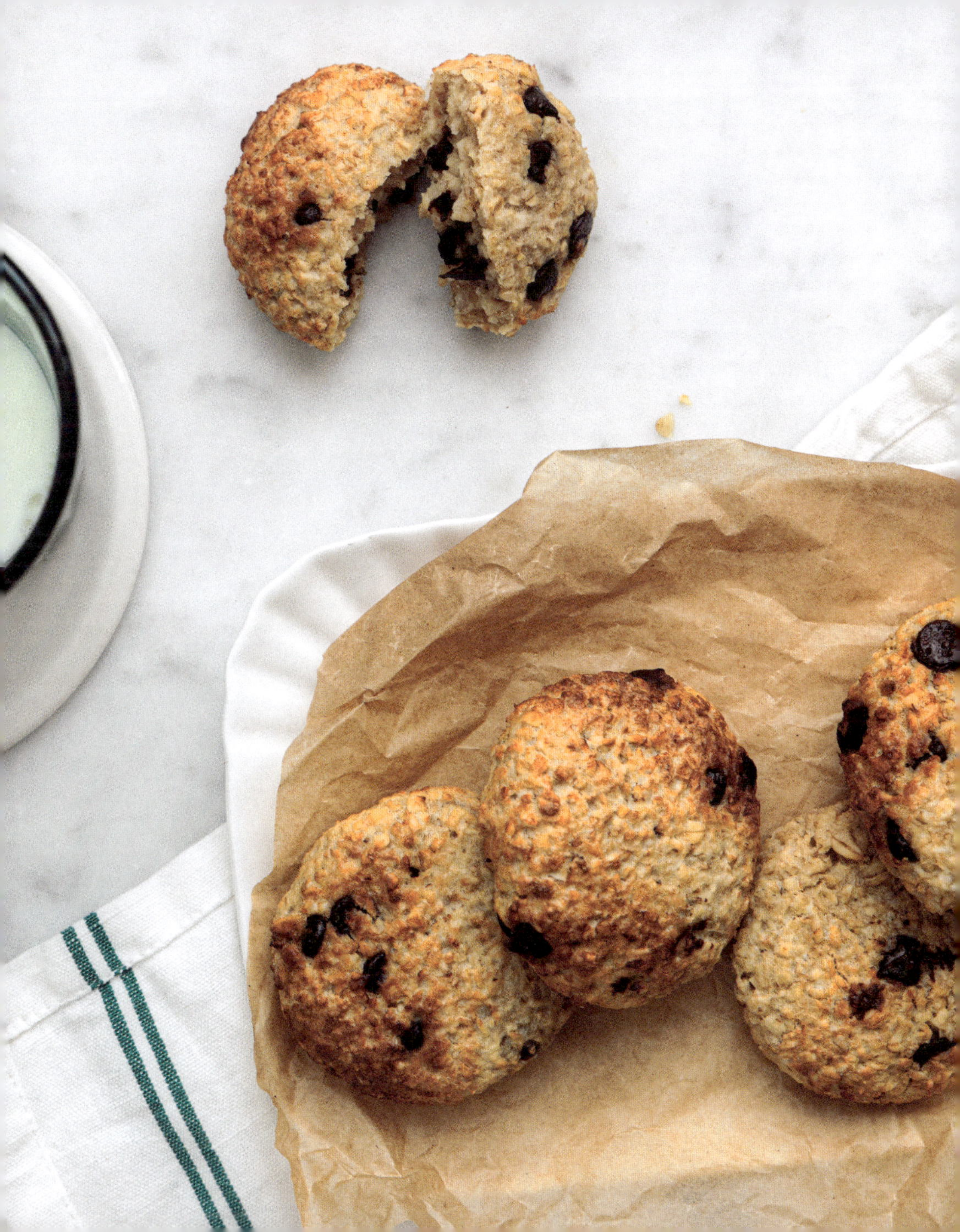

MAKES 4 - MEDIUM - PREPARATION 15 MINUTES - COOKING 10 MINUTES

FONDANT COOKIES

- 50 g (1¾ oz) dark or milk chocolate
- 1 egg
- 50 g (1¾ oz) coconut sugar or caster (superfine) sugar
- 50 g (1¾ oz) sunflower or vegetable oil or butter, melted
- 200 g (7 oz) plain (all-purpose) flour
- 60 g (2¼ oz) chocolate chips

1 Melt the chocolate in a saucepan over a low heat. On a baking tray lined with baking paper, pour the melted chocolate to create four separate rounds. Place the tray in the freezer to allow the chocolate to set.

2 In a bowl, mix the egg with the sugar and oil or melted butter, then stir in the flour. Add the chocolate chips and mix again.

3 Form eight balls of dough, flattening them slightly. Place one round of chocolate on top of four of the cookies, then cover the chocolate with the remaining four portions of dough.

4 Bake for 8 to 10 minutes at 200°C (400°F) in the air fryer pan.

DESSERT

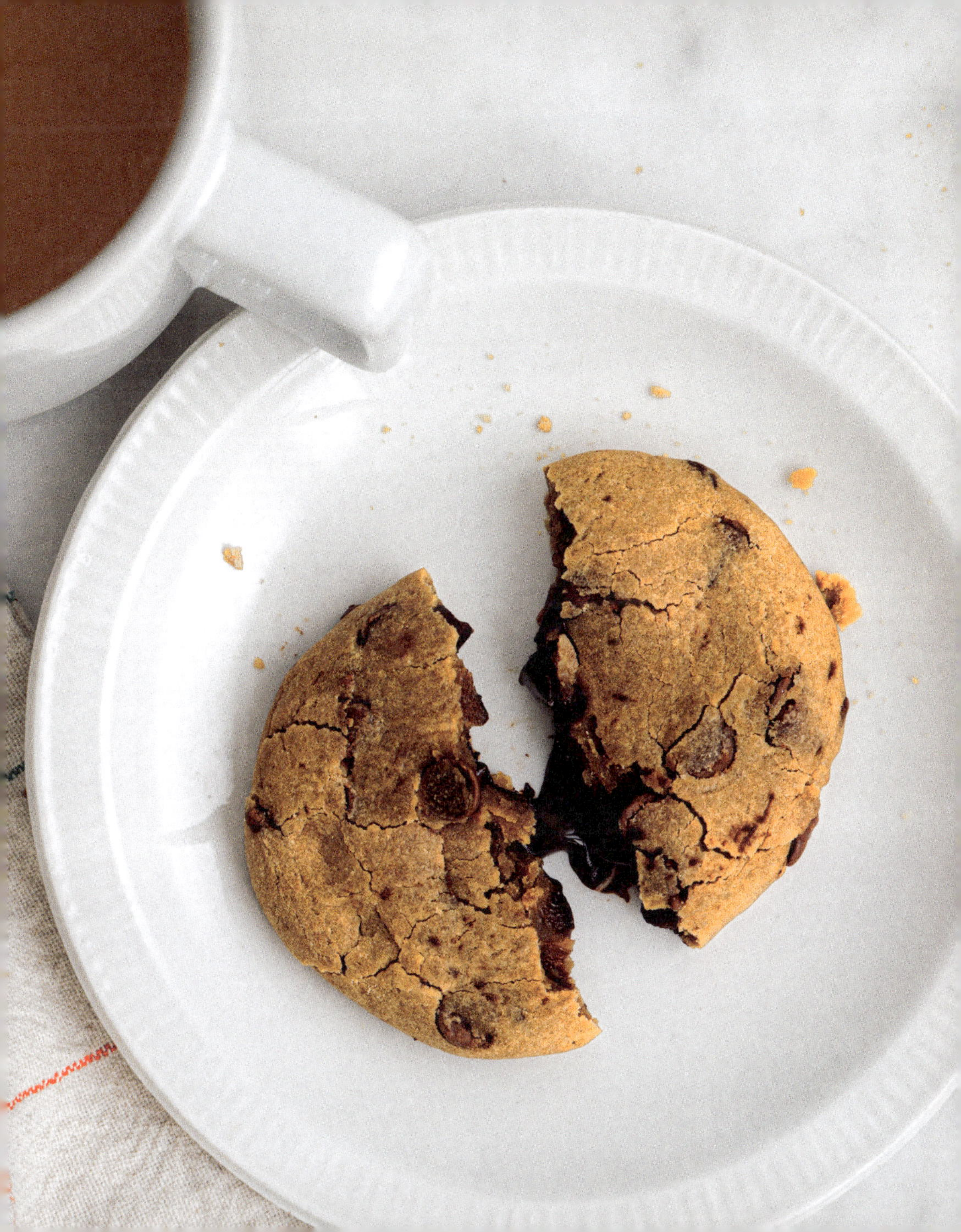

SERVES 6 - EASY - PREPARATION 15 MINUTES - COOKING 40 MINUTES

ALMOND CAKE

CAKE
- 3 eggs
- 100 g (3½ oz) quark or cream cheese
- 100 g (3½ oz) coconut sugar or caster (superfine) sugar
- 100 ml (3½ fl oz) sunflower or vegetable oil
- 200g (7 oz) plain (all-purpose) flour
- 2 teaspoons baking powder
- 100 g (3½ oz) ground almonds (almond meal)

TOPPING
- 100 g (3½ oz) ground almonds (almond meal)
- 1 tablespoon honey

1 In a bowl, mix all the cake ingredients together. Pour the batter into a greased air fryer-safe cake pan approximately 20 cm (8 inches) in diameter.

2 Mix the ground almonds with the honey and spread this mixture on top of the cake batter. Cook in the air fryer for 40 minutes at 180°C (350°F).

TIP
Add some chopped fruit — such as pear or apple — to this cake for extra flavour.

DESSERT

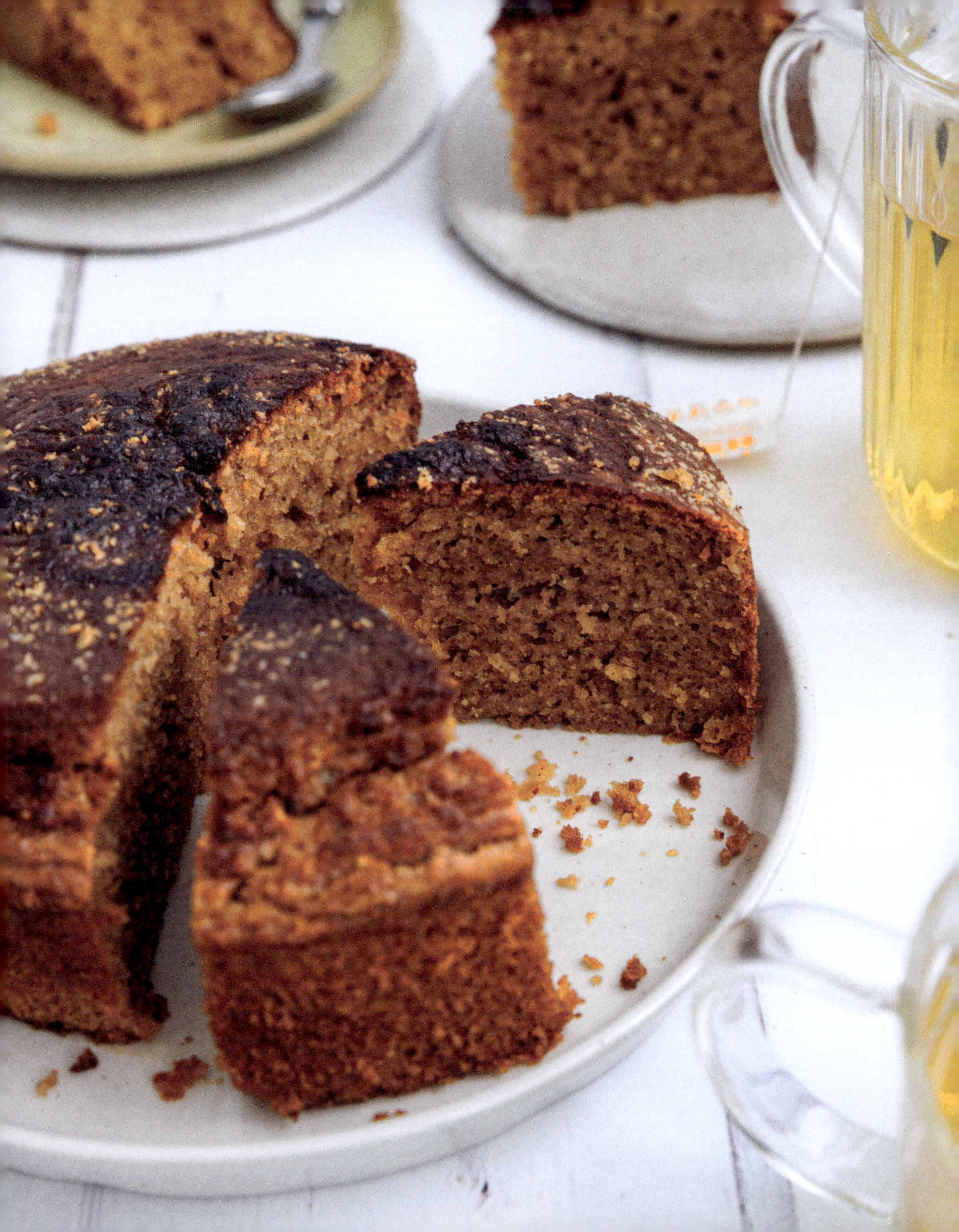

MAKES 4 - EASY - PREPARATION 15 MINUTES - COOKING 13 MINUTES

PEANUT BANANA COOKIES

- 50 g (1¾ oz) peanut butter
- 40 g (1½ oz) coconut or raw sugar
- 1 egg
- ½ banana, peeled and mashed
- 100 g (3½ oz) plain (all-purpose) flour
- 1 teaspoon baking powder
- Small pinch of salt
- 40 g (1½ oz) chocolate chips
- 30 g (1 oz) whole peanuts, finely chopped

1 In a bowl, mix the peanut butter with the sugar, then add the egg, mashed banana, flour, baking powder and salt. Once mixed, stir through the chocolate chips and chopped peanuts.

2 Place four spoonfuls of the dough into the air fryer basket and bake for 13 minutes at 190°C (375°F). Allow to cool before eating.

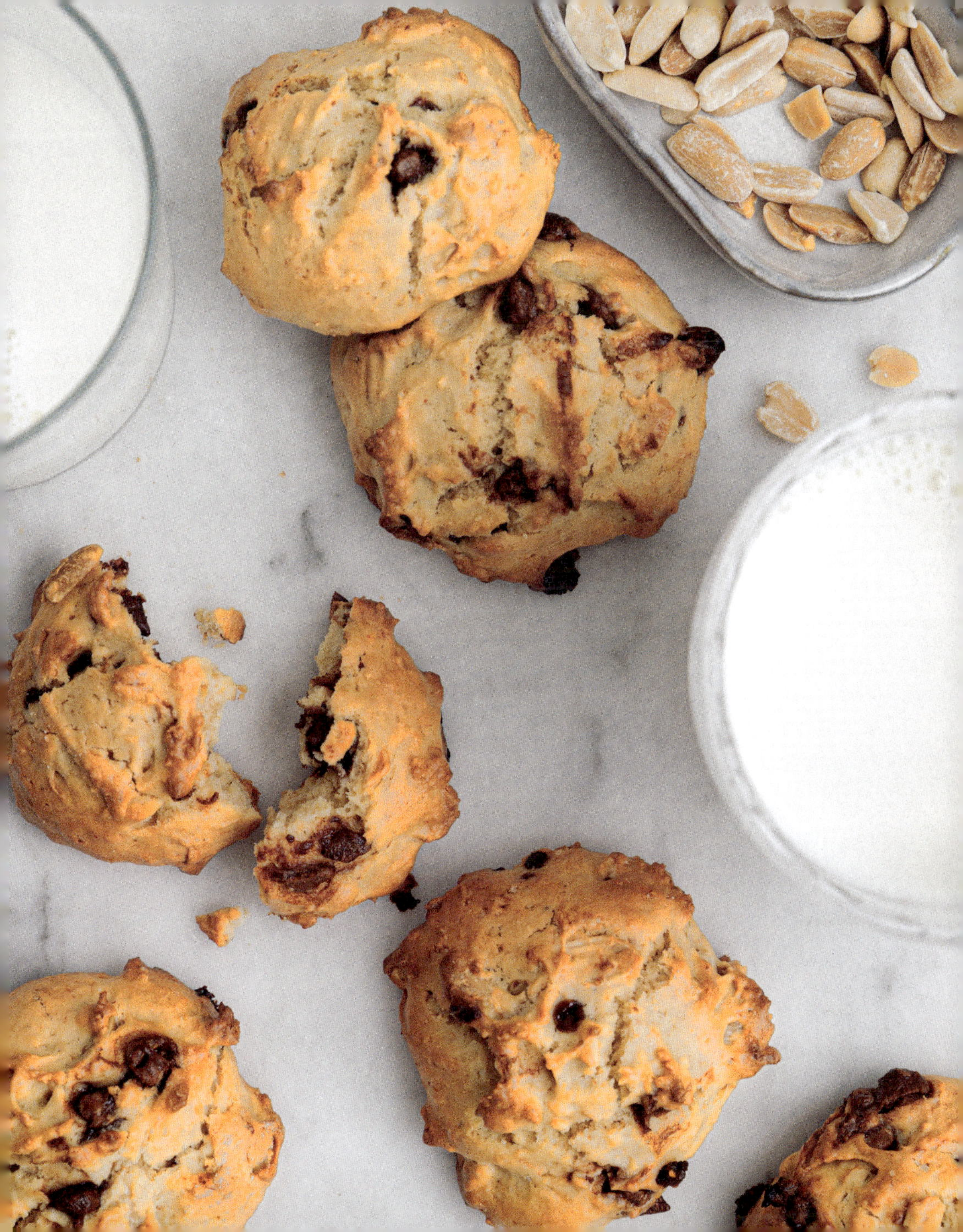

SERVES 1 - EASY - PREPARATION 10 MINUTES - COOKING 8 MINUTES

MUG CAKE

- 1 egg
- 2 tablespoons milk
- 2 tablespoons plain (all-purpose) flour
- 1 teaspoon baking powder
- 1 tablespoon apple purée
- 1 teaspoon vanilla extract or vanilla sugar (optional)
- 2 tablespoons Greek yoghurt
- 1–2 squares dark chocolate

1 In an air fryer-safe mug whisk the egg with the milk, then mix in the flour, baking powder, apple purée, vanilla or vanilla sugar and yoghurt.

2 Place the mug in the air fryer and bake for 8 minutes at 200°C (400°F).

3 Once cooked, add the chocolate squares on top. They will slowly melt.

TIP
Add some fruit on the side for a healthier treat.

DESSERT

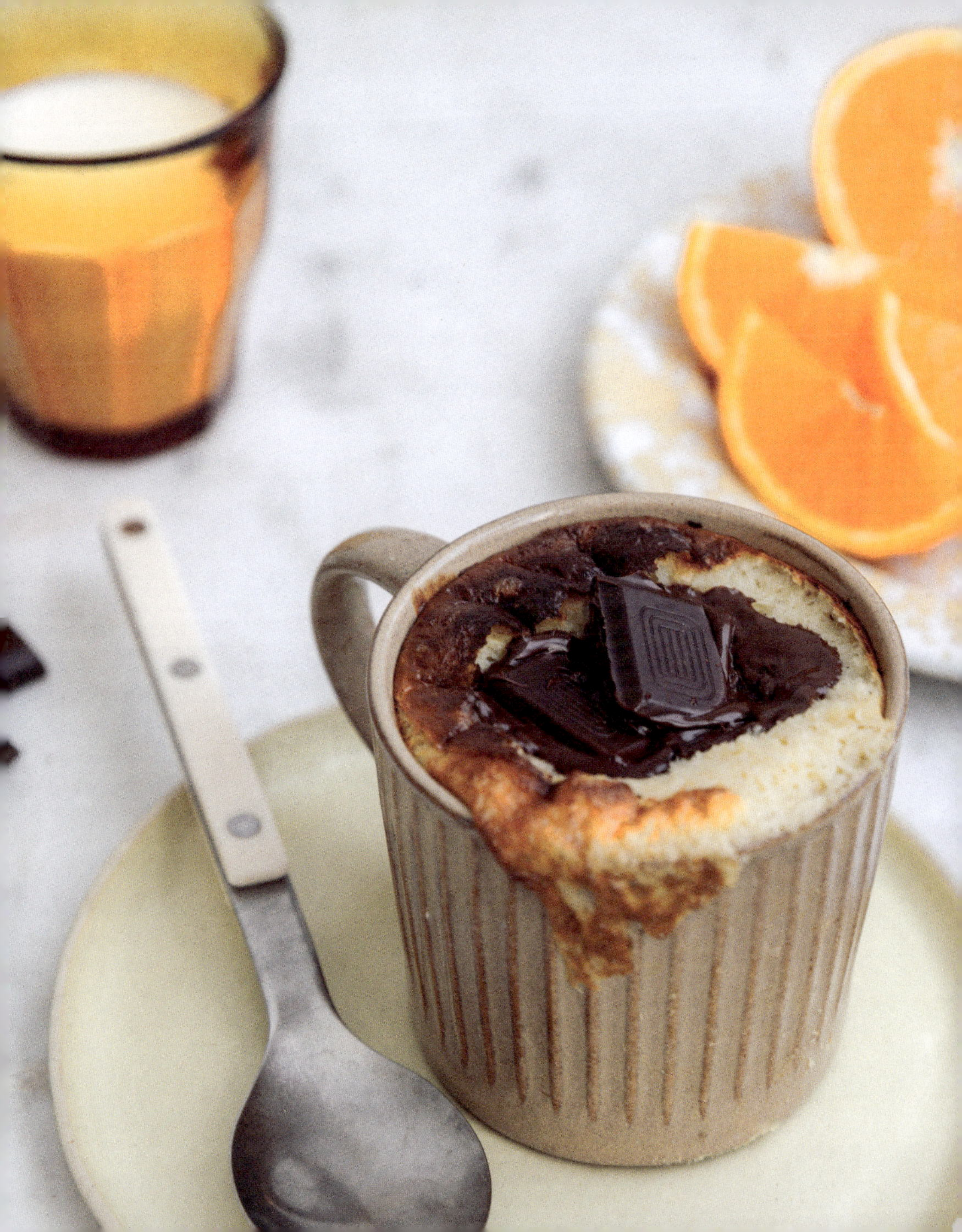

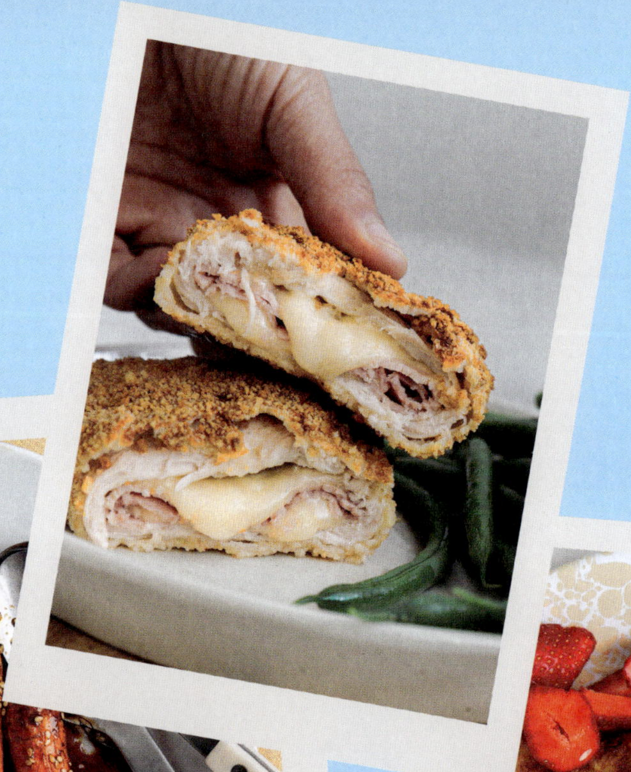
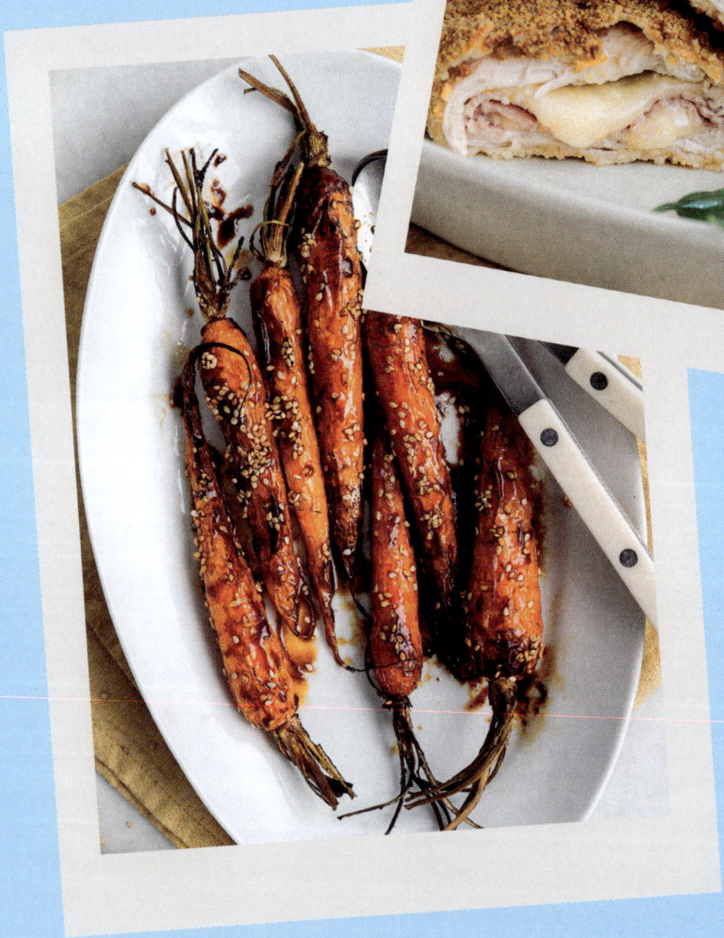
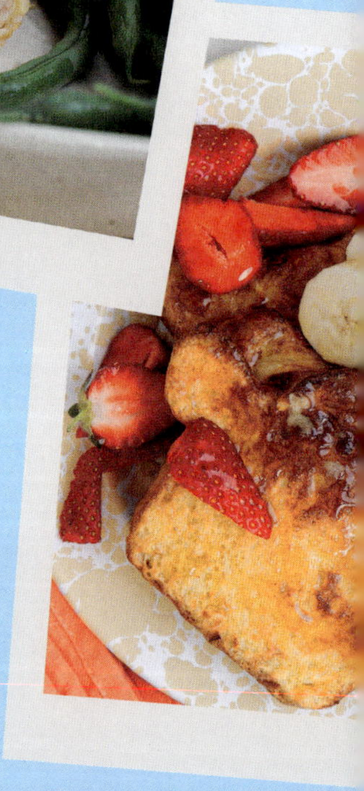

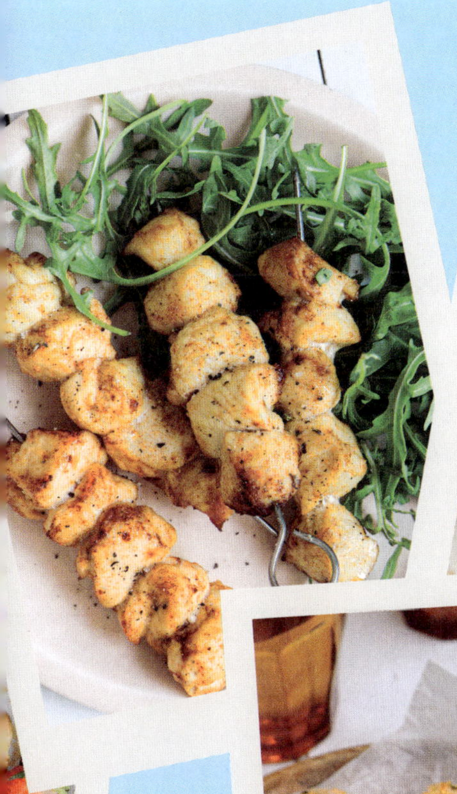
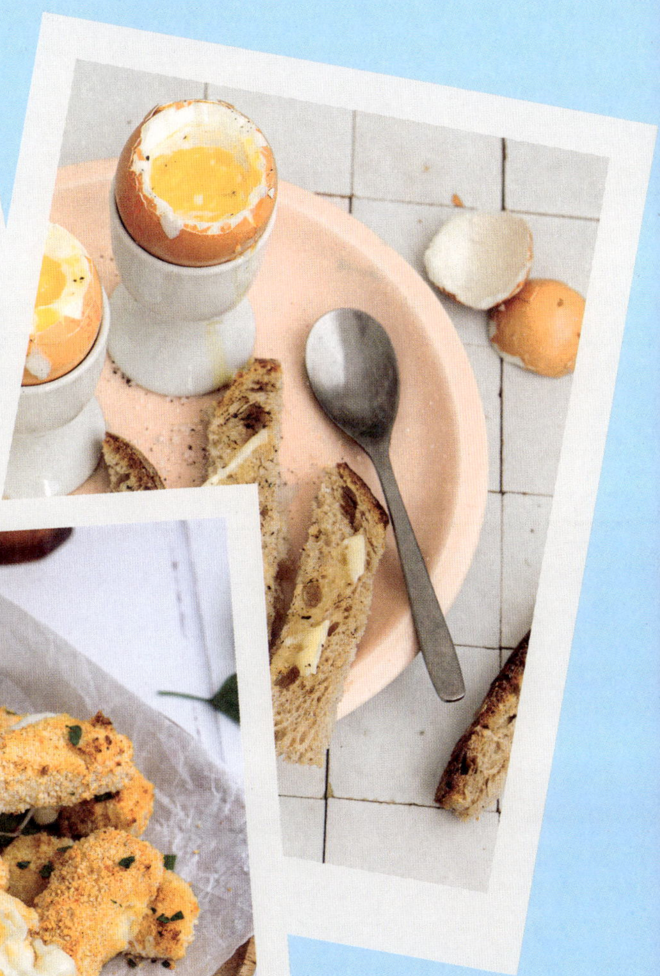
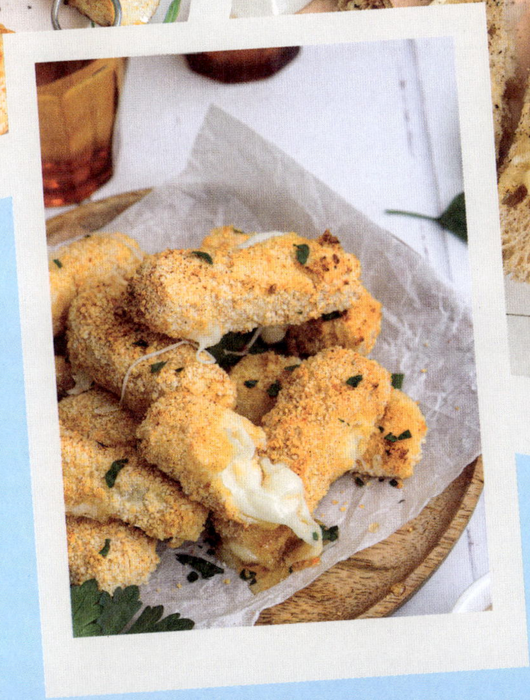
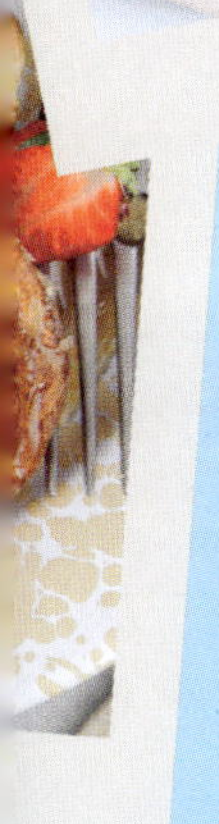

RECIPE INDEX

BREAKFAST
Boiled eggs 24
Breakfast bagel 16
Choc-banana porridge 14
Chocolate granola 18
French toast 30
Maple granola 34
Mini chocolate brioches 28
Muesli bars 20
Protein granola 26
Vegan granola 32
Vegan muffins 22

FINGER FOOD
Baked Camembert 54
Cheesy breadsticks 42
Chicken parcels 40
Mini pizza baguettes 52
Mozza sticks 48
Onion rings 44
Potato crisps 38
Pumpkin bites 46
Salted popcorn 56
Tuna triangles 50
Vegetable spring rolls 58

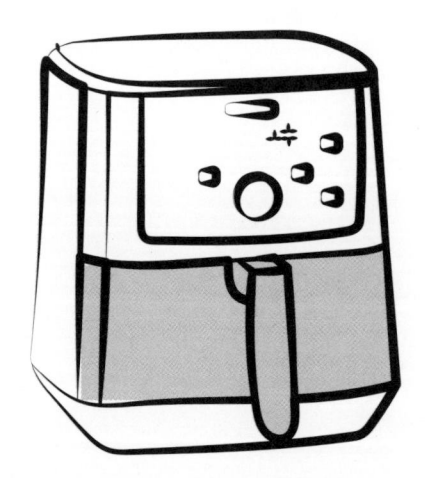

LUNCH & DINNER

Baked cod	104
Beef samosas	102
Bruschetta	90
Cheeseburgers	72
Chicken fajitas	80
Chicken nuggets	70
Cordon bleu	84
Creamy tomato and ham pasta	74
Croque madame	62
Crumbed egg yolks	92
Fish & crisps	64
Frittata with red pepper	108
Jacket potatoes	66
Meatballs	94
Mini ham croissants	86
Pistachio-crusted salmon	76
Potato rosti	94
Roasted broccoli	68
Roasted carrots	98
Roasted summer vegetables	110
Roasted vegetable fries	106
Savoury loaf	78
Smashed butternut	82
Spicy chicken skewers	100
Stuffed tomatoes	96
Veggie lasagne	88

DESSERT

Almond cake	132
Apple crumble muffins	120
Baked apples	122
Banana muffins	126
Chocolate cake	116
Chocolate chip cookies	118
Chocolate muffins	114
Fondant cookies	130
Marble cake	124
Mug cake	136
Oat cookies	128
Peanut banana cookies	134

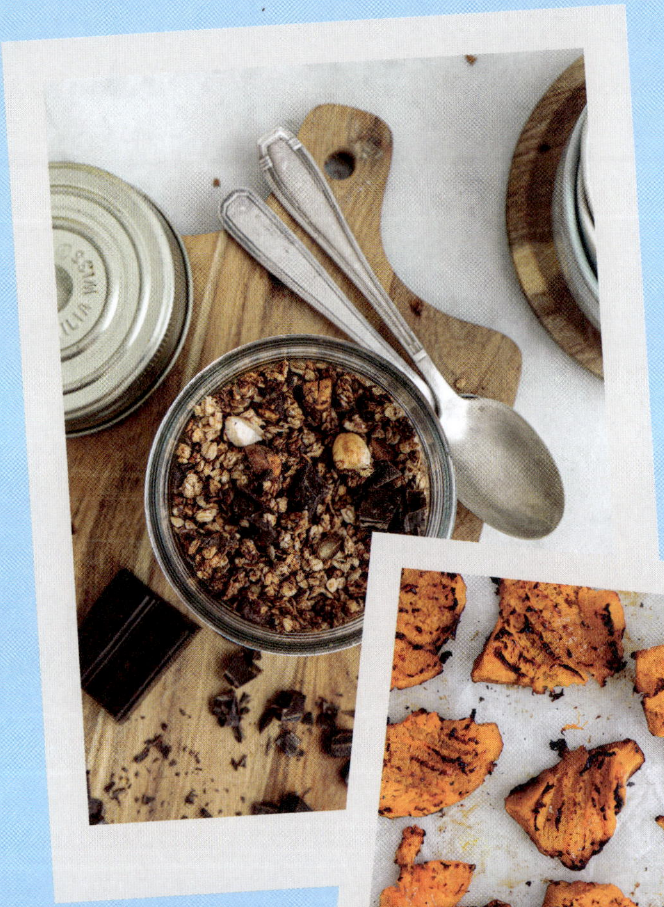
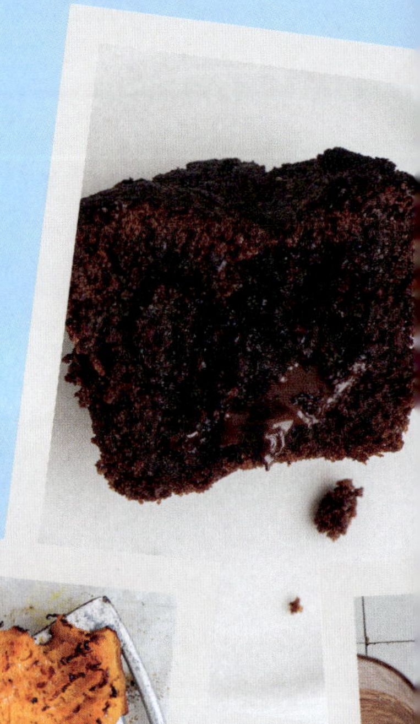
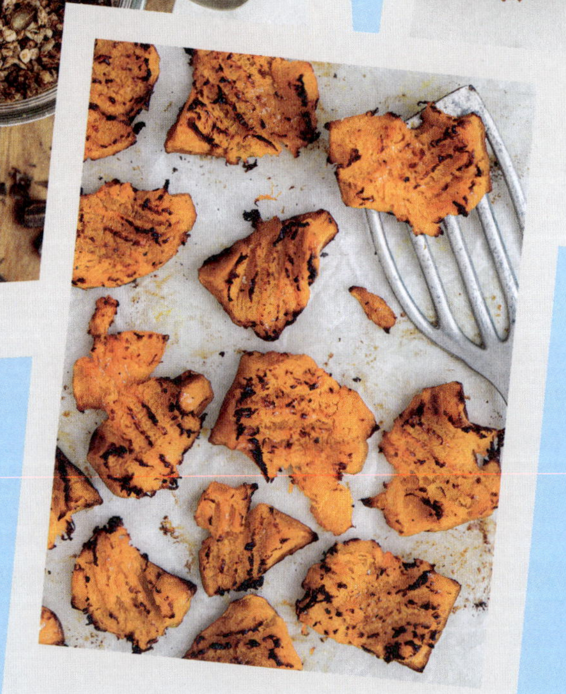
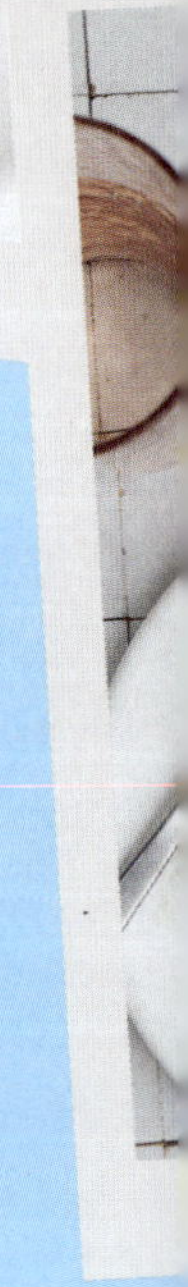

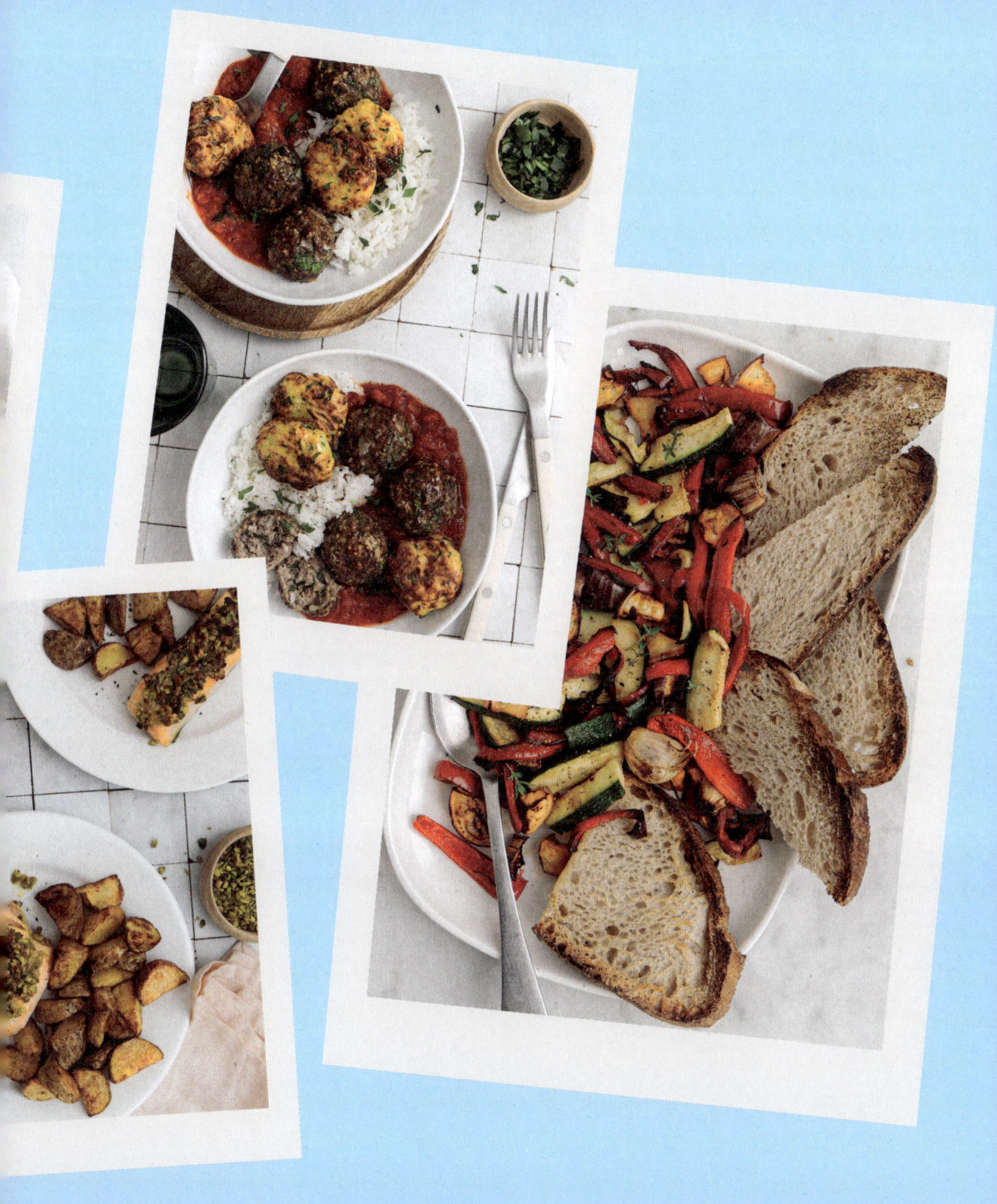

First published by Hachette Livre (Marabout) in 2024
Published in 2025 by Murdoch Books, an imprint of Allen & Unwin

Murdoch Books UK
Ormond House
26–27 Boswell Street
London WC1N 3JZ
Phone: +44 (0) 20 8785 5995
murdochbooks.co.uk
info@murdochbooks.co.uk

Publisher: Céline Hughes
Designer: Manon Renucci
Cover design: Sarah McCoy
Photographer: Lélia Castello
Stylist: Lélia Castello
Translator: Nicola Thayil
Production manager: Natalie Crouch
Text and design © Hachette Livre (Marabout) 2024

The moral rights of the author have been asserted.

All rights reserved. No part of this publication may be reproduced, stored in a retrieval system or transmitted in any form or by any means, electronic, mechanical, photocopying, recording or otherwise, without the prior written permission of the publisher.

ISBN 978 1 76150 107 4

A catalogue record for this book is available from the British Library

Printed by 1010 Printing International Limited, China

IMPORTANT: Those who might be at risk from the effects of salmonella poisoning (the elderly, pregnant women, young children and those suffering from immune deficiency diseases) should consult their doctor with any concerns about eating raw eggs.

10 9 8 7 6 5 4 3 2 1

MIX
Paper | Supporting responsible forestry
FSC® C016973